Bringing Lent Home with

Mother Teresa

Prayers, Reflections, and
Activities for Families

Donna-Marie Cooper O'Boyle

AVE MARIA PRESS AVE Notre Dame, Indiana

© 2012 by Donna-Marie Cooper O'Boyle

Founded in 1865, Ave Maria Press is a ministry of the United States Province of Holy Cross.

www.avemariapress.com

ISBN-10 1-59471-286-7 ISBN-13 978-1-59471-286-9

Cover image © Marka / SuperStock Images.

Cover and text design by Katherine Robinson Coleman.

Printed and bound in the United States of America.

Lovingly, for my children:

Justin,

Chaldea,

Jessica,

Joseph,

and

Mary-Catherine

ACKNOWLEDGMENTS

With a grateful heart to my family and friends, especially my parents, Eugene Joseph and Alexandra Mary Cooper; and my brothers and sisters, Alice Jean, Gene, Gary, Barbara, Tim, Michael, and David, I am eternally indebted. I am deeply grateful to my dear friend and "mother," Blessed Mother Teresa.

My children—I love you—Justin, Chaldea, Jessica, Joseph, and Mary-Catherine! My husband, David, the wind beneath my wings, thank you for your love and support!

Special thanks to Robert Hamma and the team at Ave Maria Press for their partnership in getting this book out to you!

INTRODUCTION

"A family that prays together stays together."

—Patrick Peyton, C.S.C., often
quoted by Mother Teresa

L ent is a distinctive journey of spiritual growth. Pope Benedict XVI tells us, "It means accompanying Jesus as he travels to Jerusalem, the place where the mystery of his passion, death and resurrection is to be fulfilled" (Wednesday audience, March 9, 2011).

The word *lent* is derived from the Anglo-Saxon word for springtime, *lencten*. As we think of the upcoming rebirth of spring, perhaps we can consider that just as the daffodil and tulip bulbs buried in the ground all winter require good soil, water, and sunshine to burst forth and brighten our spring days, so, too, fasting, almsgiving, and prayer are necessary ingredients to nurture our spiritual growth on our Lenten journey to Easter.

Blessed Pope John Paul the Great has said:

> The time of Lent is a special time for purification and penance as to allow our Savior to make us His neighbor and save us by His love. . . . The liturgical period of Lent is given us in and through the Church in order to purify us of that remainder of selfishness and excessive attachment to things, material or otherwise, which keep us apart from those who have a right to our help: principally those who, whether physically near or far, are unable to live their lives with dignity as men and women created by God in His image and likeness. (Message of His Holiness John Paul II for Lent, 1982)

Mother Teresa always affirmed the significance in living lives of sacrificial love within our homes and called everyone to be more Christlike. Her simple and practical teachings, all of which we can apply to our own lives, make her an excellent Lenten spiritual guide for families.

Your unique opportunity to retreat from the busyness of the world and carve out a bit of meaningful family prayer time within your domestic church is available right here in the pages of this book. Whether you choose the morning or evening to gather with your family (or hopefully both), your time will be well spent reflecting on the simple yet poignant bursts of inspiration and spirituality of Blessed Mother Teresa of Calcutta as well as the great traditions of holy Mother Church. You will be guided with suggestions regarding how your family can apply Mother Teresa's wisdom to your lives and how you may participate more fully with the rhythm of the Church regarding prayer, fasting, and almsgiving during a season meant to transform hearts and souls.

To use this book, simply gather your family and move page by page, day by day, making your way through Lent. You can come together morning or evening at your kitchen table, around a prayer table, or wherever you feel most comfortable. If you are gathering in the evening, you might want to use the text for the following day. Light a prayer candle if you wish. In each day you will find these elements:

Mother Teresa's Inspiration: A quotation from Blessed Mother Teresa begins the page and sets the tone for each Lenten day.

Reflection for Parents: In this section I offer you some points to ponder each day. This is for your own nourishment, but there are also some thoughts for you to share with your children. Read this reflection on your own before you gather the family together.

Family Prayer: Begin your family time together with the first prayer instruction for each day. At the end of this prayer, all say together: *Blessed Mother Mary, bring us closer to your Son, Jesus. Blessed Mother Teresa, please pray for us. Amen.* Help your children to memorize this prayer. There is another opportunity for prayer at the end of each day's meditations. Feel free to elaborate and adapt these to suit your family's needs.

A Story from Mother Teresa's Life: This booklet as a whole will tell the story of Mother Teresa's life from the earliest years and through her ministry, highlighting notable moments. This part can be read aloud by an older child or a parent.

Fasting: Each day "fasting" suggestions will be made to help guide you, the parent, and your children about what to fast from. It will not only be from certain foods, but more often will be fasting from bad habits or enjoyable activities. Although the practice of giving up one particular thing throughout Lent remains valuable, these suggestions offer additional ideas for daily fasting. Feel free to adapt them to what works best for your family.

Ash Wednesday and Good Friday are days of fasting and abstinence. Church law requires that no meat be eaten on these days by Catholics fourteen years and older. People with medical conditions, women who are pregnant, and nursing mothers are exempt from fasting and abstinence. Catholics from the age of eighteen through fifty-nine must fast on these days by only having one full meatless meal and two smaller meatless and penitential meals. The two small meals together should not equal a full meal.

Almsgiving: Each day "almsgiving" suggestions are provided to help with ideas to accomplish as a family or individually. As the season of Lent begins, ask the children if they have decided to *give up* something for Lent or if they have chosen to *do something* special to please Jesus. Have each child (with your help) write down their resolutions to be used as a reminder of what they have committed to do this Lenten season. They can hang their Lenten resolutions on their bedroom door, put them on a prayer table, or keep them in their pockets or backpacks.

All Through the Day: Each day you will be given a simple yet poignant thought to think and pray about throughout the day.

You will see that there are no entries for the Saturdays of Lent. I recommend that you use the Sunday prayers and activities throughout the weekend. The suggestions for almsgiving on Sundays may take a little longer to do and are appropriate for the weekend when there is more time.

May you all be richly blessed as your family journeys closer to heaven and its rewards through this Lenten season.

ASH WEDNESDAY

"Prayer begins by listening, God speaks in the silence of your hearts and we speak from the fullness of our hearts. I listen, God speaks. I speak, God listens. This listening, speaking is prayer."

—Mother Teresa of Calcutta

Reflection for Parents

As you gather your family today, explain to the children that during Lent we try to do three things each day. First, we give up something. This is called fasting. Second, we give something to others. This may be things we do to help others, or possessions or money we share with others. This is called almsgiving. And we pray more. While prayer, fasting, and almsgiving should be a part of our lives every day, Lent is a season for doing these things more intensely.

Mother Teresa's words remind us that God actually listens to us. This Lent, let us try to put her words into practice. Although our lives are busy, we can still seek a time of silence each day to pause, ponder, and pray.

Family Prayer

All make the sign of the cross.

> *Parent:* Dear Jesus, as we begin the season of Lent, we thank you for the example of Mother Teresa. Help us to learn from her and imitate her faith, hope, and love each day of this holy season. Now let us listen to these words of Blessed Mother Teresa.

A parent or child now reads the opening quotation aloud.

> All: Blessed Mother Mary, bring us closer to your Son, Jesus. Blessed Mother Teresa, please pray for us. Amen.

A Story from Mother Teresa's Life

Mother Teresa was born in Skopje, in what is now the Republic of Macedonia, on August 26, 1910. Even as a little girl, Mother Teresa was very aware of Jesus' love for her. She longed to love and serve him with her life in return, so she became a nun at the age of eighteen. Sister Teresa spent eighteen years as a teacher and later as headmistress (or principal) at the Loreto School in Calcutta, India.

Fasting

Discuss with your children what you as a family can offer to God as a sacrifice during Lent. Can you and the kids give up a TV show, a video game, or the Internet at times? Decide what you will all do today.

Almsgiving

Mother Teresa's words for today remind us of the importance of listening. Ask the children how they can be better listeners. Is there someone they could listen to today?

Prayer

Parent: Dear Lord, Jesus, inspire our hearts to pray more this Lent. Help us to search for the quiet moments each day.

All Pray: Blessed Mother Mary, you know the perfect way to your Son, Jesus. Teach us the way. Blessed Mother Teresa, please pray for us.

Our Father, Hail Mary, Glory Be.

All Through the Day

I will strive to find moments of silence in which to immerse my heart in prayer.

THURSDAY AFTER ASH WEDNESDAY

"Today . . . just allow Jesus to love you. We always want to say, 'Jesus, I love you,' but we don't allow Jesus to love us. Today say often, 'Jesus, I am here, love me.'"

—Mother Teresa of Calcutta

Reflection for Parents

Love, love, love! We will never fully understand Our Lord's tremendous love for us until we meet him face to face. As parents, we feel that our love for our children is immense, unconditional, and never-ending—incomparable. But, multiply that love by infinity and that will be a tiny fraction of God's love for us and our children.

Family Prayer

All make the sign of the cross.

> *Parent:* Dear Jesus, during this season of Lent, please visit us here in our home. Help us to open our hearts to the graces you wish to give us throughout this special season. Now let us listen to these words of Blessed Mother Teresa.

A parent or child now reads the opening quotation aloud.

> All: Blessed Mother Mary, bring us closer to your Son, Jesus. Blessed Mother Teresa, pray for us. Amen.

A Story from Mother Teresa's Life

On September 10, 1946, when Sister Teresa was en route to her annual retreat, she distinctly heard Jesus calling her to much more— to serve the poorest of the poor all over the world, beginning in the slums of Calcutta, India. She continued to hear the voice of Jesus calling her in her heart to leave her work at the Loreto School behind and cross the threshold to the slums of Calcutta. After consulting with her spiritual director she submitted her calling to the Church. Her proposal was approved, and on August 17, 1948, she left the Loreto convent wearing her new simple white and blue cotton Indian sari as her new religious habit. She took a medical course and on December 21, 1948, officially began her work to care for God's poor and destitute.

Fasting

What little comfort might you or the children give up today—a second serving, a dessert, a long shower?

Almsgiving

Ask the children to think of someone who is in need of love and what they could do to show love for this person. Encourage them to do this.

Prayer

Let's pray to learn to hear the voice of Jesus when he speaks within us.

> *Parent:* Dear Jesus, thank you for loving me! Mother Teresa lived each day so much in love with you, adoring you in the Eucharist and serving you in the poor. Teach me to open my heart fully to your love and hear you when you call me to love as Mother Teresa did.
>
> *All Pray:* Our Father, Hail Mary, Glory Be

All Through the Day

Jesus, I am here, love me.

"When we can't pray, it is very simple: if Jesus is in my heart, let Him pray; let me allow Him to pray in me, to talk to His Father in the silence of my heart. Since I cannot speak—He will speak; since I cannot pray—He will pray. That's why often we should say: 'Jesus in my heart, I believe in your faithful love for me; I love you.'"

—Mother Teresa of Calcutta

Reflection for Parents

Mother Teresa tells us straight out that prayer isn't always easy. Sometimes it's downright hard. Sometimes we don't know how to pray or even if we can pray at all. Mother Teresa experienced this too. She went through an extremely long "dark night of the soul." St. John of the Cross described this as a spiritual crisis, trouble praying, feelings of abandonment by God, or a sense of loneliness and desolation. Mother Teresa lets us in on a simple solution: pray anyway! Express our love to Jesus. Give him everything, especially our inadequacies.

Family Prayer

All make the sign of the cross.

> *Parent:* Dear Lord, during this Lent, help us to believe in your great love for us. Please come into our hearts and grant us an increase in faith today. Now let us listen to these words of Blessed Mother Teresa.

A parent or child now reads the opening quotation aloud.

> *All:* Blessed Mother Mary, bring us closer to your Son, Jesus. Blessed Mother Teresa, pray for us. Amen.

A Story from Mother Teresa's Life

The religious order that Jesus instructed Blessed Teresa to start was called the Missionaries of Charity and was officially established on October 7, 1950. Because Sister Teresa founded the order, she was referred to as Mother Teresa. Mother Teresa understood that it was necessary to deepen her prayer life so that she could properly carry out the difficult work of caring for the unwanted, lepers, the sick, and the dying. She felt it a privilege to be able to participate in the holy sacrifice of the Mass each morning and said it was "one of the greatest gifts." When she was not actively involved with the poor, she spent much time praying in adoration of Jesus in the Blessed Sacrament.

Fasting

Ask the children if they can give up a little time today, just ten minutes. They can give it to God in prayer or help a sibling or parent in some way.

Almsgiving

Assist the kids to be more helpful today by telling them to focus on offering their help without being asked.

Prayer

Let us pray today for all those in our family who may be sick (*name them*).

> *Parent*: Dear Lord, you love us even when we don't know how to pray properly. Please accept the simple prayers of our hearts. *All say*: "Jesus, I love you."

> *All pray*: Our Father, Hail Mary, Glory Be

All Through the Day

Jesus in my heart, I believe in your faithful love for me; I love you.

"If you are humble nothing will touch you, neither praise nor disgrace, because you know what you are. If you are blamed you will not be discouraged. If they call you a saint you will not put yourself on a pedestal."
—Mother Teresa of Calcutta

Reflection for Parents

Today is the First Sunday of Lent. All of the gospels for the Church's three-year cycle of readings (Mt 4:1–11, Mk 1:12–15, Lk 4:1–13) focus on Jesus' temptation by the devil in the desert. The devil, as we know, tried to get Jesus to bow down and worship him. Jesus, of course, would not fall for his traps.

Mother Teresa's words help us to see that we should not fall into sin due to the temptation to be praised or the temptation to be discouraged. She teaches us that the virtue of humility will guard us from the temptation to be honored and praised. There were many occasions in Mother Teresa's life in which she could have fallen prey to the devil's temptations. But Mother Teresa chose to remain humble through prayer and thus accepted all praise and awards she received in the name of the poor, including the Nobel Peace Prize. She gave all glory to God.

Mother Teresa remained grounded in prayer to prevent falling into discouragement or despair when things were difficult, and things often were, as she regularly faced heartrending conditions and desperate poverty among the people she served.

Family Prayer

All make the sign of the cross.

Parent: Dear Lord, please hear our prayers voiced from humble hearts. Please be with us as we gather this day to give glory to you. Now let us listen to these words of Blessed Mother Teresa.

A parent or child now reads the opening quotation aloud.

All: Blessed Mother Mary, bring us closer to your Son, Jesus. Blessed Mother Teresa, pray for us. Amen.

A Story from Mother Teresa's Life

Mother Teresa told the story of an unexpected and precious gift she received late one night. The doorbell rang and Mother Teresa opened the door to find a poor man standing there shivering from the cold. He told Mother Teresa that he heard she had just received the Nobel Peace Prize and wished to also give her a prize. With that, he handed her a small offering of money that was really everything he had. Mother Teresa said she was more moved by this humble man's generosity than she was by the prestigious Nobel Peace Prize.

Fasting

During the upcoming week, fast from the situations that may cause you to become proud. Offer kind words and encouragement to others. Explain to the children that it is okay to feel happy about doing well, but resist getting overly puffed up about accomplishments and never consider themselves better than someone else. Help the children think of an accomplishment of someone else that they want to praise or congratulate him or her for and to plan to do that soon.

Almsgiving

Ask the children if they have a toy or article of clothing they are willing to donate to the local thrift shop or homeless shelter. Plan a day this upcoming week for you and your children to bring a donation to a collection point. If you feel ambitious, consider arranging a collection of used clothing at your parish sometime during these forty days of Lent to be given to a homeless shelter, the St. Vincent de Paul Society, or the Missionaries of Charity.

Prayer

Let us pray today for our Holy Father, priests, and religious.

Parent: Dear Lord, help us to learn from Mother Teresa as we journey through Lent this week. Please guide us together in prayer each day in our homes and help us to be a radiant example to our community.

All Pray: Our Father, Hail Mary, Glory Be

All Through the Day

Teach us to be humble, Lord.

MONDAY, FIRST WEEK OF LENT

"[It is] not how much you give, but how much love you put in the giving."

—Mother Teresa of Calcutta

Reflection for Parents

So often we worry that we have to accomplish so much. It is only natural to feel this way; we usually have very long to-do lists. But Mother Teresa shows us another way to view our actions. She wants us to focus on love rather than on the number of accomplishments. Our Lord wants our love, not our lists. Knowing this can bring us incredible peace in our hearts.

Family Prayer

All make the sign of the cross.

> *Parent:* Dear Lord, during this special season of Lent increase the love in our hearts and grant us the graces we need to act more lovingly and sincerely, and to seek out those in need. Now let us listen to these words of Blessed Mother Teresa.

A parent or child now reads the opening quotation aloud.

> *All:* Blessed Mother Mary, bring us closer to your Son, Jesus. Blessed Mother Teresa, pray for us. Amen.

A Story from Mother Teresa's Life

One time when Mother Teresa was visiting her sisters at a convent in the United States, she appeared very happy after coming out of the bathroom. One of the sisters questioned her about her obvious delight. Mother Teresa replied that she felt that a sister there must really love Jesus. She said that when she saw how sparkling clean the bathroom was she thought that the sister assigned to cleaning it was doing her task with great love to please Jesus. This made her very happy.

Fasting

Along with your children, consider if there is a bad habit you need to work on correcting. Perhaps this is a day to try and work on it. Talk to the children about being less irritable and more loving today. It's a good day to fast from being grumpy or uncharitable.

Almsgiving

Challenge the children to do whatever they should do today with love, trying to please Jesus in everything. Whether it's eating all of their vegetables, being polite and treating everyone with respect, helping with something around the house, tidying up their rooms, or sharing their toys, it will please Jesus when done with love.

Prayer

Let us pray today that our work, our play, and all our actions become like prayers that are pleasing to God.

> *Parent*: Dear Jesus, help us to try to do everything with love, even the very menial tasks, knowing that is what pleases you.

> *All (read together or repeat after the parent)*: I am sorry for the times I have been unloving and selfish. I will do all my tasks today as lovingly and as well as I possibly can to please you, Lord.

> *All Pray*: Our Father, Hail Mary, Glory Be

All Through the Day

Our Lord wants our love, not our lists.

"We must give until it hurts. For love to be true it has to hurt. It hurt Jesus to love us; it hurt God to love us because He had to give. He gave His Son. This is the meaning of true love, to give until it hurts."

—Mother Teresa of Calcutta

Reflection for Parents

Mother Teresa was all about love. She loved the poorest of the poor and all whom she met with Christ's gentle love. Her life of service remains an amazing example to all of us. Beyond that, she also preached love with her words whenever she had the opportunity. Her words challenge us to love more deeply—to actually love *sacrificially*.

Family Prayer

All make the sign of the cross.

> *Parent*: Dear Jesus, during this Lent teach each of us in our family how to sacrifice for the betterment of others. Now let us listen to these words of Blessed Mother Teresa.

A parent or child now reads the opening quotation aloud.

> *All*: Blessed Mother Mary, bring us closer to your Son, Jesus. Blessed Mother Teresa, pray for us. Amen.

A Story from Mother Teresa's Life

Mother Teresa often taught that real giving happens when it hurts. She said too many times people only give of their surplus and don't sacrifice at all when giving. She told the story of meeting a beggar one day. She said the beggar told her that he knew others had donated to her for the poor and he also wanted to give. He stretched out his hand and offered twenty-nine *paise*, which is not enough to buy much of anything. For a moment, Mother Teresa felt torn since she didn't want to take his food money and cause the beggar to go hungry. It was everything he received from begging that day. She decided to accept it and observed an immediate radiance of joy come across the man's face. His tiny contribution became like thousands to Mother Teresa because it was given with love and sacrifice.

Fasting

Talk to the children about loving until "it hurts" as Mother Teresa taught. This can be put into action today by doing something that is inconvenient or unpleasant, such as helping with chores when they would rather watch TV or play a game.

Almsgiving

Suggest to the children that they befriend someone at school or in the neighborhood who seems to be unpopular, explaining that they will be demonstrating God's love to them in the spirit of Mother Teresa.

Prayer

Let us pray today for those who make sacrifices for us (*each one names somebody*).

> *Parent*: Dear Jesus, teach us how to love as Mother Teresa suggests. Help us to give until "it hurts."

All Pray: Our Father, Hail Mary, Glory Be

All Through the Day

"Any sacrifice is useful if it is done out of love."

"Do ordinary things with extraordinary love."
—Mother Teresa of Calcutta

Reflection for Parents

It may not always be so simple to strive to do ordinary things with extraordinary love. We can be in such a rush most days. We may want to zip right through things rather than to put in the extra effort, the extra love. We may also consider the ordinary things to be, well, *ordinary*. Yet therein lies a mystery within the ordinary. As we learn more about Mother Teresa and many of the saints, we discover that graces abound in the ordinariness that makes up so much of our lives.

Family Prayer

All make the sign of the cross.

> *Parent*: Dear Jesus, be with us today as we pray as a family. Please grant us the graces to always strive to go about our daily lives with extraordinary love. Now let us listen to these words of Blessed Mother Teresa.

A parent or child now reads the opening quotation aloud.

> *All*: Blessed Mother Mary, bring us closer to your Son, Jesus. Blessed Mother Teresa, pray for us. Amen.

A Story from Mother Teresa's Life

Anyone who spent time with Mother Teresa was usually struck by the joy that radiated from her. I experienced this myself with her and with her sisters as well. Mother Teresa explained that joyfulness is at the heart of the Missionaries of Charity. She encouraged all to radiate the joy of Jesus always and to express it in their actions.

Mother Teresa actually told the sisters that if they can't be joyful with the poor they may as well pack up and go home, because the depressed don't need to see gloomy faces and get more depressed. The poor need to feel loved, she said. The sisters lead lives of deep prayer and ask Jesus to work through them. They do ordinary things with extraordinary love.

Fasting

Doing ordinary things with extraordinary love takes a little more time. Discuss with the children how you can all give up rushing through a chore today and spend a bit more time doing it with care.

Almsgiving

Suggest to the children that they take a few minutes today to think about someone at school, in the family, or the neighborhood who could benefit from a small act of kindness. See if you can help them to carry it out, either today or sometime soon.

Prayer

Let us pray today for our teachers and all who work at our schools.

> *Parent*: Dear Lord, Jesus, thank you for your extraordinary love for us. Our love is so meager in comparison. Even though ours will never be equal to yours, teach us to love more *extraordinarily*.

> *All pray*: Our Father, Hail Mary, Glory Be

All Through the Day

Jesus wants me to "do ordinary things with extraordinary love."

"Be kind and merciful. Let no one ever come to you
without coming away better and happier."
—Mother Teresa of Calcutta

Reflection for Parents

As parents, Mother Teresa's words remind us of the Scripture
passage: "Is there anyone among you who, if your child asks
for bread, will give a stone? Or if the child asks for a fish, will give a
snake?" (Mt 7:9–11).

We naturally want our children to come away from us better and
happier. That's precisely one of the reasons why you are making this
family Lenten journey—for the betterment of your children's spiritual lives, and with God's grace, their happiness in heaven. Beyond
your family, our Lord calls you through Mother Teresa's words to be
looking out for the betterment of others too.

Family Prayer

All make the sign of the cross.

> *Parent*: Dear Lord, help us to be open to your graces
> and message for us today and each day of Lent. Now
> let us listen to these words of Blessed Mother Teresa.

A parent or child now reads the opening quotation aloud.

> *All*: Blessed Mother Mary, bring us closer to your
> Son, Jesus. Blessed Mother Teresa, pray for us. Amen.

A Story from Mother Teresa's Life

Mother Teresa told a story about a little girl she taught when she
was at the Loreto School. She said the six-year-old girl was naughty
and seemed very selfish. One day when the girl was being extremely

naughty, Mother Teresa decided to take her by the hand and go for a walk with her. Mother Teresa said the girl held onto her hand with one hand and she tightly held her money in her other hand, all the while saying that she wanted to buy this or that.

They never did go to a store. Instead, they came upon a blind beggar and immediately the little girl let open her grasp of the money, putting it into the beggar's hands. Mother Teresa said the experience completely changed the girl who from that day forward was kind, obedient, and loving.

Fasting

Ask the children if they can resist saying anything unkind today, especially if someone is unkind to them.

Almsgiving

Ask the children to show a special kindness to a classmate or family member today. It would be particularly special if they could show kindness to someone who is grumpy or uncaring.

Prayer

Today let us pray for one of our classmates who especially needs our prayers.

> *Parent*: Dear Lord, Jesus, Mother Teresa has taught that no one should ever come to us without coming away better and happier. Please help us to be generous and loving people.

> *All (read together or repeat after the parent)*: Help us to be kind and merciful, Lord.

> *All pray*: Our Father, Hail Mary, Glory Be

All Through the Day

"Be kind and merciful."

FRIDAY, FIRST WEEK OF LENT

"Our Lord, on the cross, possessed nothing. He was on the cross which was given by Pilate. The nails and crown were given him by the soldiers. He was naked, and when he died, cross, nails, and crown were taken away from him. And he was wrapped in a shroud given him by a kind man and buried in a tomb which was not his."

—Mother Teresa of Calcutta

Reflection for Parents

On Fridays in Lent it's beneficial to meditate upon Christ's passion and death. Mother Teresa's words drive home the point that our Lord had nothing and, further, in his nothingness, he redeemed the world! Those are significant words to ponder today. We can think about Christ's great love for us and his willingness to suffer a humiliating death on the cross for our sins.

Family Prayer

All make the sign of the cross.

> *Parent*: Dear Lord, Jesus, while we are here on earth we most likely will never fathom your great love for us and your great suffering for us. Please grant us the graces to be more prayerful this Lent and to be especially sorry for our sins. Now let us listen to these words of Blessed Mother Teresa.

A parent or child now reads the opening quotation aloud.

> *All*: Blessed Mother Mary, bring us closer to your Son, Jesus. Blessed Mother Teresa, pray for us. Amen.

A Story from Mother Teresa's Life

Mother Teresa and Pope Paul VI knew one another and were close spiritually. The pope was always interested in the progress of the Missionaries of Charity and had advised Mother Teresa regarding the government of the order. Mother Teresa was struck by the pope's words when he described the great pain he experienced because of arthritis. He had said, "I just live my Mass." She knew his suffering was not just physical though; he suffered great emotional pain over things that were happening in the Church at the time. Mother Teresa explained that we—every one of us—should live our Mass all through the day by offering our sufferings, our joys, and our challenges to God, leaving them all at the foot of the cross in prayer.

Fasting

Ask the children to take a couple of minutes today and think about a time they were disobedient or unkind, and how they could do better next time.

Almsgiving

In light of the fact that everything was given to Jesus on the cross, ask the children to give Jesus ten minutes today in some way, perhaps by helping or praying for someone.

Prayer

Today let us pray for someone whom we have hurt by our words or actions.

Parent: Dear Lord, forgive us our sins.

All (read together or repeat after the parent): We love you!

All pray: An Act of Contrition, Our Father, Hail Mary, Glory Be

All Through the Day

Lord, I am sorry for my sins. I love you!

SECOND SUNDAY OF LENT

"One thing Jesus asks of me: that I lean upon Him; that in Him and in Him alone I put my complete trust; that I surrender myself to Him unreservedly. I need to give up my own desires in the work of perfection. Even when all goes wrong, and I feel as if I was a ship without a compass, I must give myself completely to Him."

—Mother Teresa of Calcutta

Reflection for Parents

Today is the Second Sunday of Lent. All of the gospels for the Church's three-year cycle of readings speak about the transfiguration of Jesus (Mt 17:1–9, Mk 9:2–10, Lk 9:28–36). Jesus took Peter, James, and John up a high mountain and revealed his glory to them. His face began shining like the sun and his clothes were a dazzling pure white. From a cloud a voice said, "This is my beloved Son, with whom I am well pleased; listen to him" (Mt 17:5).

The disciples were overcome with fear and fell down. Jesus comforted them, telling them to get up and not to be afraid. When they traveled back down the mountain, Jesus told them not to reveal what had happened to anyone until after he rose from the dead. Peter, James, and John were privileged with an incredible holy experience to strengthen them for the journey ahead.

In her words, Mother Teresa explained that perhaps the most important thing Jesus asked of her was to lean on him and trust in him. She said, "Even when all goes wrong," she would give herself completely to him. When everything in her spiritual life had the appearance of being wrong and she no longer experienced the consoling presence of Jesus as she once had, she trusted in Christ. Jesus had prepared her for this journey with many graces and the certainty that he was indeed directing her in her ministry. Jesus calls all of us to lean on him completely no matter what things may seem like, no matter how we feel.

Family Prayer

All make the sign of the cross.

> *Parent:* Dear Jesus, be with us today and help us to lean on you for everything. Now let us listen to these words of Blessed Mother Teresa.

A parent or child now reads the opening quotation aloud.

> *All:* Blessed Mother Mary, bring us closer to your Son, Jesus. Blessed Mother Teresa, pray for us. Amen.

A Story from Mother Teresa's Life

Shortly after Mother Teresa began her work, she started to feel an inner loneliness deep in her soul. The inner voice she had heard calling her to start the order had stopped and she seemed to be alone. Her prayers felt dry and almost useless; her heart was heavy. She experienced feelings of abandonment, like Jesus on the cross.

Nonetheless, Mother Teresa continued to put one foot in front of the other in faith each day to care for the poor and remain faithful to her prayer life, no matter how difficult it was or how empty she felt. She also continued to smile at everyone and did not complain. Jesus had strengthened her to endure this suffering just as he did with his apostles in the transfiguration.

Mother Teresa stayed true to her word: "One thing Jesus asks of me: that I lean upon Him; that in Him and in Him alone I put my complete trust."

Fasting

Consider with your children the idea of "fasting" as much as possible from popular culture today. No magazines, television, Internet, radio, and shopping malls. Sound radical? Try it! Enjoy a peaceful, prayerful, loving Sunday together.

Almsgiving

Is there someone in your family, neighborhood, parish, or community who is struggling with some sort of challenge? Create a greeting card with the children and include a comforting message even as simple as "Jesus loves you!" Mail the card or drop it off in the person's mailbox. If time does not permit today, perhaps another day, and, for today, lift that person up in prayer.

Prayer

Parent: Let us pray today for all the members of our family. *Ask the children to pray by name for someone (e.g., a grandparent, aunt, uncle, or cousin) whom they want to pray for.*

Dear Lord, we love you and trust you with our lives.

All pray: Our Father, Hail Mary, Glory Be

All Through the Day

Jesus wants me to lean on him and trust him wholeheartedly.

MONDAY, THE SECOND WEEK OF LENT

"Jesus comes to us in the form of bread to show us His love for us, and He makes Himself the hungry one so that we can feed Him. He is always there, the hungry one, the homeless one, and the naked one."
—Mother Teresa of Calcutta

Reflection for Parents

As parents, we certainly meet Jesus every day in our children. God has put us within our domestic church to help work out the salvation of our children, our spouses, and ourselves. Countless opportunities for grace are offered each day. Hidden within the care of the family or household chores, our Lord presents many encounters and experiences for us. It is up to us to decide to respond in love to everything we face. He will give us the strength and courage when we ask.

Family Prayer

All make the sign of the cross.

> *Parent*: Please open our hearts to hear you calling us to respond in love to the many people you put in our midst during this season of Lent. Now let us listen to these words of Blessed Mother Teresa.

A parent or child now reads the opening quotation aloud.

> *All*: Blessed Mother Mary, bring us closer to your Son, Jesus. Blessed Mother Teresa, pray for us. Amen.

A Story from Mother Teresa's Life

Mother Teresa conferred often with Pope Paul VI and they were close spiritual friends. In 1964, Pope Paul took part in an international Eucharistic Congress in Bombay. He decided to donate the white Lincoln car that had been donated to him for his visit to Bombay to the Missionaries of Charity. Mother Teresa was very grateful for the pope's gift; however, neither she nor her sisters ever rode in the car. Instead, she raffled it off and used the proceeds to care for the lepers. Whenever she received any prize or gift, she would immediately think about how she could use it to benefit the poor.

Fasting

Talk with the children about fasting from judging someone today. Mother Teresa explains that Jesus comes to us in all of the "undesirables" of society. We should never judge them.

Almsgiving

Can you "regift" something today or this week? Following the mindset of Pope Paul VI and Mother Teresa, perhaps there is someone who could benefit from the item even more than you.

Prayer

Today, let's pray for all of the unwanted and lonely people in the world, that God would put someone near them to bring them comfort.

> *Parent*: Dear Lord, Jesus, please use me to be a comfort to others, even with a loving smile. Remind me to rise to every occasion with love.

> *All pray*: Our Father, Hail Mary, Glory Be

All Through the Day

"Jesus comes to meet us." I will welcome him in everyone.

TUESDAY, THE SECOND WEEK OF LENT

"It is not what we do, but how much love we put in the doing, and to whom we are doing it, that is the important thing. . . . to be constantly available to Him . . . no matter in what form He may come to us."

—Mother Teresa of Calcutta

Reflection for Parents

Raising a family means we have to be ready for anything, as Mother Teresa suggests. It could be a sudden illness, an injury, a sibling rivalry, financial difficulties, or something more serious. In those crazy or chaotic moments we handle the situation with prayer, often followed by a big sigh. Hopefully, we realize that we need not try to do too much or do everything. Rather let us focus on all that our good Lord decides to give us, even those things we feel may be insurmountable. With his grace, we will get through as we serve God through our families.

Family Prayer

All make the sign of the cross.

> *Parent*: Dear Lord, thank you for the gift of our family. Open our hearts to one another today, throughout this season of Lent, and always. Now let us listen to these words of Blessed Mother Teresa.

A parent or child now reads the opening quotation aloud.

> *All*: Blessed Mother Mary, bring us closer to your Son, Jesus. Blessed Mother Teresa, pray for us. Amen.

A Story from Mother Teresa's Life

Mother Teresa was totally united in spirit to Jesus and prayed constantly. She said, though, that she had often wondered about what her life would be like living with the contemplative sisters and away from the world, concentrating only on Jesus. But Mother Teresa said she realized early on that she could be totally happy and in love with Jesus out in the world and that was where he was calling her to be, to serve the poor and meet him in them. She said she lived with Jesus twenty-four hours a day. Like Mother Teresa we, too, can be prayerful people and live holy lives by praying throughout our daily activities, pleasing God and bringing people closer to him.

Fasting

Can you fast from worrying today? God does not want us to worry. He wants us to give him all of our concerns and fears in prayer.

Almsgiving

Explain to the children that today they can offer God any worry, fear, or concern that comes to their minds. Do they have a friend or classmate who worries or is fearful? Ask the children to say a prayer for them.

Prayer

Today, let us pray for families all over the world, especially for families who are struggling in some way.

Parent: Dear Lord, Jesus, thank you for loving us. Please let your love shine through us to others. Please take care of families everywhere.

All pray: Our Father, Hail Mary, Glory Be

All Through the Day

We must be convinced that when we serve others, we are serving Jesus.

WEDNESDAY, THE SECOND WEEK OF LENT

"Thoughtfulness is the beginning of great sanctity. . . .
Our vocation, to be beautiful, must be full of thought for
others. . . . Jesus went about doing good. Our Lady did
nothing else at Cana but thought of the needs of others
and made their needs known to Jesus."

—Mother Teresa of Calcutta

Reflection for Parents

Mother Teresa teaches us that "thoughtfulness is the beginning
of great sanctity." Sometimes being thoughtful is as simple as
smiling at your spouse, your children, or your neighbor, or being
cheerful even when things are tough and you are feeling a bit "off."
Smile anyway. You never know what kind of positive effect it will
have on others—and on you!

Family Prayer

All make the sign of the cross.

> *Parent:* Dear Lord Jesus, help us to remember that you
> want us to think of others before ourselves. Now let
> us listen to these words of Blessed Mother Teresa.

A parent or child now reads the opening quotation aloud.

> *All:* Blessed Mother Mary, bring us closer to your
> Son, Jesus. Blessed Mother Teresa, pray for us. Amen.

A Story from Mother Teresa's Life

One time while attending a meeting, Mother Teresa was asked
to give a little inspirational message. She stood up and looked out at
the group and simply said that husbands should smile at their wives
and wives should smile at their husbands and children. Someone

wondered how she could give this advice and asked her, "Are you married?" She replied that she certainly was married—to Jesus—and sometimes she found it difficult to smile at Jesus because he could be so demanding!

Fasting

Ask the children if they can fast from complaining today. Suggest to them that they be extra thoughtful and think before they speak, which will aid them in trying not to complain.

Almsgiving

Challenge the children to give away at least ten beautiful smiles today and then to whisper a little prayer to Jesus for the people they have smiled at. They can keep track of the smiles by drawing a smiley face on a piece of construction paper for each time they have sincerely smiled at someone. For the younger ones, you can draw the faces and they can color them in once they have passed on their sweet smiles.

Prayer

Today, let's pray for those who have not been treated with thoughtfulness. Let us pray also for those who are victims of war.

Parent: Dear Lord, Jesus, help us to take on a spirit of thoughtfulness and love.

All pray: Our Father, Hail Mary, Glory Be

All Through the Day

"Thoughtfulness is the beginning of great sanctity."

THURSDAY, SECOND WEEK OF LENT

"How much we can learn from our Lady! She was so humble because she was all for God. She was full of grace. . . . She is sure to tell us, 'Do whatever he tells you.'"

—Mother Teresa of Calcutta

Reflection for Parents

Are we "all for God"? Let's ponder today how we live our lives and how we might live them more like Mary. Our Blessed Mother's trust in her God and her humility and love speak to us as parents. Mary, although full of grace and the mother of Jesus, was human like us and needed to decide to be unwavering in her faith, much the same as we should. She is a wonderful example of virtue for us to emulate.

Family Prayer

All make the sign of the cross.

> *Parent*: Dear Lord, please grant us the graces to become humble like Mary in service to you. Now let us listen to these words of Blessed Mother Teresa.

A parent or child now reads the opening quotation aloud.

> *All*: Blessed Mother Mary, bring us closer to your Son, Jesus. Blessed Mother Teresa, pray for us. Amen.

A Story from Mother Teresa's Life

Mother Teresa loved the Blessed Mother and actually kept company with her constantly through prayer. She depended on Mary for help with her work and to draw others close to Jesus. She taught her sisters to pray constantly, especially the rosary. Mother Teresa was always seen with her beads quietly gliding through her fingers even as she sat in meetings or when conversing with people.

Her devotion to Mary was simple yet sublime. She encourages us to get closer to Mary. She teaches us to trust in Mary's intercession and allow Mary to become our mother. One time when I was on complete bed rest due to a precarious pregnancy, Mother Teresa taught me a simple prayer: "Mary, Mother of Jesus, be a mother to me now."

Fasting

Suggest to the children that they fast today from unkind thoughts about others and from saying unkind things.

Almsgiving

Ask the children to think about a gift they can give to the Blessed Mother today—a prayer, a gesture, an act of kindness, a sacrifice.

Prayer

Let us pray for families all around the world. (Try to plan a time today or sometime soon to gather the family to pray a decade of the rosary for this intention.)

> *Parent*: Dear Lord, Jesus, thank you for the blessing of our family.
>
> *All (read together or repeat after the parent)*: "Mary, Mother of Jesus, be a Mother to me now."
>
> *All pray*: Our Father, Hail Mary, Glory Be

All Through the Day

I will do whatever God tells me to do today. I will strive to be like Mary.

"We need silence to be alone with God, to speak to him, to listen to him, to ponder his words deep in our hearts. We need to be alone with God in silence to be renewed and to be transformed. Silence gives us a new outlook on life. In it we are filled with the grace of God himself, which makes us do all things with joy."

—Mother Teresa of Calcutta

Reflection for Parents

Silence? Yes, silence. Mother Teresa's suggestion of silence for prayer may seem impossible for parents of active families. Yet it is in the silence that we will hear God's whispers to our souls. Instead of waiting for a perfectly still household where prayer would be easier, perhaps we should go down a bit deeper into our hearts when we pray. Perhaps we should take advantage of even the briefest moments of silence to raise our hearts to God in prayer. It is in the journey to the depths of our hearts in prayer that we will find the silence in which the Lord can speak.

Family Prayer

All make the sign of the cross.

> *Parent*: Dear Lord, help us to find quiet moments today in which to pray. Now let us listen to these words of Blessed Mother Teresa.

A parent or child now reads the opening quotation aloud.

> *All*: Blessed Mother Mary, bring us closer to your Son, Jesus. Blessed Mother Teresa, pray for us. Amen.

A Story from Mother Teresa's Life

One time Mother Teresa was visited by a group of Hindu children who had traveled far to see her. At school they had won prizes and traded them in for money. They asked to be brought to Mother Teresa so that they could give her the money for the poor. This delighted Mother Teresa. She knew that the children could have easily used the money on themselves, but had chosen to help the poor with all of the money they had earned.

Fasting

Encourage your children to fast from noise today. Ask them to give up a television show, a video game, or a noisy activity and instead spend the time being quiet and prayerful.

Almsgiving

Depending on how well they do with their fasting, you might want to reward your children with a monetary prize and encourage them to do what the Hindu children did—offer it to the poor in some way.

Prayer

Let us pray for the poor today who depend on the generosity of others.

> *Parent*: Dear Lord, Jesus, please take care of the poor and be generous to those in need.

> *All pray*: Our Father, Hail Mary, Glory Be

All Through the Day

I will seek some form of silence today to get closer to God.

THIRD SUNDAY OF LENT

"Be careful of all that can block that personal contact with the living Jesus. The devil may try to use the hurts of life and sometimes your own mistakes to make you feel it is impossible that Jesus really loves you, is really cleaving to you. This is a danger for all of us. And so sad, because it is completely opposite of what Jesus is really wanting, waiting to tell you. Not only that He loves you, but even more—He thirsts for you."

—Mother Teresa of Calcutta

Reflection for Parents

Today is the Third Sunday of Lent. The gospels for the Church's three-year cycle of readings are each different, but they all invite us to a conversion of heart and to remember the words of Ash Wednesday: "Turn away from sin and be faithful to the Gospel."

Jesus invited the Samaritan woman (Jn 4:5–42) to repent of her sin and drink of the Living Water for a true conversion. Jesus cleansed the temple (Jn 2:13–25) and forcefully ejected the money changers. Finally, Jesus gives us the example of the barren fig tree (Lk 13:1–9) as an example of God's great patience with us even when we fail.

Mother Teresa's words today speak to us about the danger of obstacles blocking us from changing our hearts and maintaining "a personal contact with the living Jesus." These hindrances can be sin in our life or holding onto a hurt or grudge. Jesus invites us to release them all to him in prayer and ask for his forgiveness and healing and allow him to love us.

Family Prayer

All make the sign of the cross.

Parent: Dear Lord, please draw our family closer to you. Help us to understand your great love for us. Forgive us of our sins. Thank you for your unending love. Now let us listen to these words of Blessed Mother Teresa.

A parent or child now reads the opening quotation aloud.

All: Blessed Mother Mary, bring us closer to your Son, Jesus. Blessed Mother Teresa, pray for us. Amen.

A Story from Mother Teresa's Life

Mother Teresa often spoke about our call to holiness—all of us. Mother Teresa told her sisters that to become holy doesn't mean we will be doing extraordinary things, but rather "consists in accepting, with a smile, what Jesus sends us. It consists in accepting and following the will of God." The key words here are *smile* and *accepting*. We often struggle to accept God's will when we are called to endure challenging situations. Mother Teresa makes it clear that we must not only accept God's will, but go one step further. God calls us even to smile, to be thankful and trust him to know exactly what we need. Mother Teresa's instructions can bring us peace and help us recognize this secret path to fulfillment and holiness.

Fasting

Discuss with your children what you can offer to God as a sacrifice during the upcoming week. Can you all give up a TV show, a video game, or the Internet at times throughout the week?

Almsgiving

With the surplus of time you have gained by giving up some of the various media, can you take time to make a phone call to a lonely relative, visit a neighbor, or make amends with someone whom you may not have spoken with in a while? Encourage your children to be good helpers and lend a hand to each other at home with chores and homework. Can you schedule time to just *be* together this week—to play a board game or have a meaningful conversation?

Prayer

Parent: Let us pray today for our pastor as well as any other priests or deacons in our parish. Dear Lord, we allow many things to get in the way of realizing your love for us. Getting caught up in the routines and busyness of our lives, we forget that you are longing for our love. We offer you our busy lives, our worries, our mistakes, and our sins and ask you to forgive us and bless us. Help us to thirst for your love as you thirst for ours.

All Pray: Our Father, Hail Mary, Glory Be

All Through the Day

Jesus thirsts for my love!

MONDAY, THIRD WEEK OF LENT

"When we look at the cross, we realize how He loved us — only love could have made Him do that. When we look at the tabernacle, we know how He loves us now. He loves you and He loves me. He made Himself Bread of Life to satisfy our hunger for His love."

—Mother Teresa of Calcutta

Reflection for Parents

You are making your way through Lent with many reminders from Mother Teresa about how much Jesus loves you and how much he wants to love you more through your conversations with him and time spent with him adoring him in the Blessed Sacrament—all of which will bring a deep sense of peace to your heart and a closer union with Jesus.

Family Prayer

All make the sign of the cross.

> *Parent:* Dear Lord, come close to us as we pray. Be always in our thoughts and with us in all our activities. Now let us listen to these words of Blessed Mother Teresa.

A parent or child now reads the opening quotation aloud.

> *All:* Blessed Mother Mary, bring us closer to your Son, Jesus. Blessed Mother Teresa, pray for us. Amen.

A Story from Mother Teresa's Life

Mother Teresa was told many times that she was very courageous to do the work that she did. She was humble and received all this praise in Jesus' name. Mother Teresa explained that if she wasn't totally convinced that Jesus was present in each and every person she cared for, each body of a leper that reeked with a foul stench, each abandoned child in dire need, each alcoholic, and so on, then she couldn't possibly do the work.

Jesus' love gave her the courage. She said Christ whom she received in the Eucharist each morning at Mass, and whom she adored in the Blessed Sacrament each day, was the same Jesus she touched in each and every one of the forsaken poor. Mother Teresa had no doubt about it.

Fasting

Ask the children to think about "fasting" today from selfishness. Help them to ask where they might be acting selfish (by not sharing, not loving, or not accepting an unpopular student at school or a kid in the neighborhood). Explain to them that Jesus lives within all of us and asks us to serve him in some way.

Almsgiving

Encourage the children to give to someone today in an unselfish way.

Prayer

Let us pray in thanks for the presence of Jesus in the Eucharist. (Try to bring the children for a visit to the Blessed Sacrament today or at some time soon, if possible.)

> *Parent*: Dear Lord, Jesus, thank you for your great love for us. Help us to be courageous enough to share that love with others.
>
> *All pray:* Our Father, Hail Mary, Glory Be

All Through the Day

God loves me with great tenderness.

"When Christ said: 'I was hungry and you fed me,' he didn't mean only the hunger for bread and for food; he also meant the hunger to be loved. Jesus himself experienced this loneliness. He came among his own and his own received him not, and it hurt him then and it kept hurting him. The same hunger, the same loneliness, the same having no one to be accepted by and to be loved and wanted by. Every human being in that case resembles Christ in his loneliness; and that is the hardest part, that's real hunger."

—Mother Teresa of Calcutta

Reflection for Parents

Just as Mother Teresa lived her life by the Parable of the Sheep and the Goats in the Gospel of Matthew (25:31–46), so should we. This scripture passage meant so much to Mother Teresa that she went around preaching it whenever she could. Holding up her hand with the five fingers extended she would say these five words while closing each finger: "You-did-it-to-me." As a parent, do you see Jesus in your children, in your spouse? Can you strive to see him there and treat him with tender love and compassion today?

Family Prayer

All make the sign of the cross.

> *Parent*: Dear Lord, please help us to see that whatever way we treat one another, we are treating you. Now let us listen to these words of Blessed Mother Teresa.

A parent or child now reads the opening quotation aloud.

> *All*: Blessed Mother Mary, bring us closer to your Son, Jesus. Blessed Mother Teresa, pray for us. Amen.

A Story from Mother Teresa's Life

Mother Teresa's work with the poor attracted many observers no matter how humbly and quietly she operated. It was obvious to onlookers that her ministry to the poor was very special. One time a Hindu man told Mother Teresa that she and he both did social work but the difference was that he did it for *something* and she did it for *someone*. Mother Teresa pointed out that she and the sisters try to do their work as beautifully as possible, always seeking to serve Jesus in each person with great love, respect, and compassion.

Fasting

Ask the children to think of one way they might fast from negativity, perhaps by turning away from a negative influence, not listening to it, deciding not to watch television today, or not listening to gossip.

Almsgiving

Encourage the children to think of others before themselves all day today.

Prayer

Let us pray today for the hungry, the thirsty, and all the poor. (Teach the children to make the same gesture as Mother Teresa with their hand and say the words: "You-did-it-to-me.")

> *Parent*: Open our hearts, dear Lord, to the "hungry" in our lives.

> *All pray*: Our Father, Hail Mary, Glory Be

All Through the Day

God wants me to seek out the "hungry" today and every day.

WEDNESDAY, THIRD WEEK OF LENT

"Joy is not simply a matter of temperament. In the service of God and souls, it is always hard to be joyful—all the more reason why we should try to acquire it and make it grow in our hearts. Joy is prayer; joy is strength; joy is love; joy is a net of love by which we catch souls."

—Mother Teresa of Calcutta

Reflection for Parents

You certainly will not always feel joyful. Life is sometimes very demanding. Yet Mother Teresa suggests that joy is an integral part of our spiritual lives and tells us that we should allow it to grow in our hearts. Children will thrive in the joyful love of their parents. How can you make your joy grow today? Can you seek it out even amid difficulties? Ask God to help you allow it to grow so that it can be a radiance in your soul that will attract others to your Christianity.

Family Prayer

All make the sign of the cross.

> *Parent*: Dear Lord, during this Lent help us to see the deep joy in our lives and be able to share it with others. Now let us listen to these words of Blessed Mother Teresa.

A parent or child now reads the opening quotation aloud.

> *All*: Blessed Mother Mary, bring us closer to your Son, Jesus. Blessed Mother Teresa, pray for us. Amen.

A Story from Mother Teresa's Life

Mother Teresa often said that she was totally convinced that each time she or her sisters helped the poor, they really were offering help to Jesus. That is why they do it with great joy. I have experienced this great joy of the sisters and Mother Teresa myself. It's contagious and lovely. Mother Teresa often told the sisters that the poor have enough troubles and reasons to feel depressed. They don't need a sad or despondent sister ministering to them. So, instead, the sisters are bursting with joy and smiling faces. That alone is a great medicine.

Fasting

Ask the children to fast from complaining and grumbling today. There is far too much to be joyful about and thankful for.

Almsgiving

Encourage the children to pay someone a compliment today. Remind them that a compliment shows their appreciation for a good quality in another person and helps them both to be joyful.

Prayer

Let us pray today for those who have been affected by a natural disaster. (*If possible, mention something current.*)

> *Parent*: Dear Lord, Jesus, please take care of our family and all those you have brought close to us—neighbors, friends, classmates, and teachers.

> *All pray*: Our Father, Hail Mary, Glory Be

All Through the Day

Jesus wants to fill my heart with joy to give to others.

"Love begins at home, love lives in homes and that is why there is so much suffering and so much unhappiness in the world today, because there is so little love in the homes and in family life. . . . If we are to bring that love again, we have to begin at home. We must make our homes centers of compassion and forgive endlessly."

—Mother Teresa of Calcutta

Reflection for Parents

A parent's role in the family and Mother Teresa's role with the poor are really very similar. A parent's actions of care for the family are not merely caring for exteriors, but also, and sometimes more importantly, the interiors—the hearts and souls of the children. The beautiful blessedness of living in a family is the call to help one another to work out our salvation within the home with love and forgiveness. What three things can you do today that will make your home a place of compassion and forgiveness?

Family Prayer

All make the sign of the cross.

> *Parent*: Thank you, dear Lord, for Your love for us. Thank you for our family. Now let us listen to these words of Blessed Mother Teresa.

A parent or child now reads the opening quotation aloud.

> *All*: Blessed Mother Mary, bring us closer to your Son, Jesus. Blessed Mother Teresa, pray for us. Amen.

A Story from Mother Teresa's Life

Mother Teresa once said that she and her sisters have never accepted an invitation to go out to eat—never. The simple reason is that she never wanted to take anything in return for her free and loving work for the poor, not even a glass of water. This may seem very radical, but we need to consider that she was a woman of great sensibility and deep faith and love. Her respect for the poor was so immense that she knew she needed to set that important example for us. She didn't want any confusion about the fact that all of their services were offered with prayer and love—no strings attached.

Fasting

Talk to the children about fasting from fighting and arguing today. If they are feeling especially argumentative, they can say a prayer instead of stirring up trouble.

Almsgiving

Encourage the children to offer their help to someone today in some way. Some ideas include helping a classmate at school, helping a sibling, helping a parent, or helping with chores without being asked.

Prayer

Today let us pray for our president and all world leaders.

Parent: Dear Lord, Jesus, help our family to work together and to remain united in love and in prayer, and in so doing, be a light to others around us.

All pray: Our Father, Hail Mary, Glory Be

All Through the Day

I will look for opportunities today to make my home a center of compassion and forgiveness..

"How much we need Mary to teach us what it means to satiate God's thirsting Love for us which Jesus came to reveal to us."

—Mother Teresa of Calcutta

Reflection for Parents

The Blessed Mother will teach us so much. Mother Teresa learned to stand with Mary at the foot of the cross, so very close to her Son, Jesus. There she listened with Mary to the painful cry of Jesus, "I thirst." Mary can help teach us how to quench Christ's thirst—his thirst for our love and the love of our family. Let us call upon Mary often for help with raising our families and for guidance in getting closer and closer to Jesus.

Family Prayer

All make the sign of the cross.

> *Parent*: Dear Jesus, thank you for your holy Mother Mary. Help us this Lent to stand with her at your cross and to pray to her more. Now let us listen to these words of Blessed Mother Teresa.

A parent or child now reads the opening quotation aloud.

> *All*: Blessed Mother Mary, bring us closer to your Son, Jesus. Blessed Mother Teresa, pray for us. Amen.

A Story from Mother Teresa's Life

One time Mother Teresa taught a lesson by speaking about electrical wires and how the current passes through them. Without the current, there is no electricity, she explained. She said the current is

God and we are the wires that must allow the current to pass through us. By allowing Jesus to pass through our wire, we allow light to come through, and by refusing, we permit darkness. Mother Teresa said the Blessed Mother was the best wire of all because she surrendered her life completely to God and allowed him to fill her totally with grace. Mother Teresa explained that at the moment when Mary conceived Jesus she ran in haste to help her cousin Elizabeth. Mother Teresa encourages us all to be like Mary and allow Jesus to work through us.

Fasting

Encourage the children to fast from technology as best they can today; even some is better than nothing.

Almsgiving

Along with the children, offer a decade of the rosary today, or this week, for your family's growth in holiness and in thanksgiving for the gift of your Catholic faith.

Prayer

Today, let us pray for all mothers, especially those who are pregnant, that their unborn babies will be blessed and lead healthy lives.

Parent: Dear Lord, Jesus, we love you.

All pray: Our Father, Hail Mary, Glory Be

All Through the Day

Lord, help me quench your thirst for my love.

"Let us all become a true and fruitful branch on the vine Jesus, by accepting him in our lives as it pleases him to come: as the Truth, to be told; as the Life, to be lived; as the Light, to be lighted; as the Love, to be loved; as the way, to be walked; as the joy, to be given; as the Peace, to be spread; as the sacrifice, to be offered, in our families and our neighbors."

—Mother Teresa of Calcutta

Reflection for Parents

Today is the Fourth Sunday of Lent. The gospel readings for three cycles of Lent offer perspectives on Jesus, the Light of the World. They are the stories of the man born blind (Cycle A), Jesus meeting Nicodemus at night (Cycle B), and the prodigal son (Cycle C).

The man born blind (Jn 9:1–41) receives his sight—both physically and spiritually—while those around him seem "blind" and lacking in faith. His story speaks to us about faith. In the parable of the prodigal son (Lk 15:1–3, 11–32), the wayward son sees the error of his ways, he sees the "light," while his brother seems to be "blind" to his own selfishness and his father's mercy. In the story about Nicodemus (Jn 3:14–21), Nicodemus sought out Jesus in the night, fearful that he would be seen with Jesus, but nonetheless was drawn to the light of Christ. Jesus told Nicodemus: "But whoever lives in truth comes to the light, so that his works may be clearly seen as done in God."

Mother Teresa's simple yet compelling words focus on instructing us how to allow Jesus to come into our lives. She suggests that we accept Jesus as truth, life, light, love, joy, peace, the way, and the sacrifice—all to be given to others in the way that pleases him. By truly living in the light of Jesus through prayer and the sacraments we can radiate his light and be a source of love and comfort for our families and beyond.

Family Prayer

All make the sign of the cross.

> *Parent:* Dear Jesus, You are the vine; we are the branches. Allow us to become a true and fruitful branch on your vine. Now let us listen to these words of Blessed Mother Teresa.

A parent or child now reads the opening quotation aloud.

> *All:* Blessed Mother Mary, bring us closer to your Son, Jesus. Blessed Mother Teresa, pray for us. Amen.

A Story from Mother Teresa's Life

Soon after Blessed John Paul II became the pope, Mother Teresa traveled to Rome. At a general audience when Mother Teresa was suddenly in front of him, she bowed, holding Pope John Paul II's right hand in both of her hands, and kissed his ring—a gesture of deep love and reverence.

Pope John Paul II was very much moved at Mother Teresa's public act of commitment and in response, immediately bent down and planted a kiss on the top of Mother Teresa's head. The image of that encounter was captured by photographers and appeared in the newspapers the following day.

The two became fast friends, and Mother Teresa and Pope John Paul II met together many times to discuss the Church and her work with the poor. An onlooker would be struck by their contrasts: he in regal vestments and she dressed in an incredibly simple cotton sari. What they shared unmistakably in common, though, was the *light* that radiated from them. They lived in Christ's light and offered it to the world.

Fasting

Spend a few minutes talking to the children about their plan for fasting this week.

Almsgiving

Is there a particular person the children would like to focus on this week who can use some cheering up or some sort of assistance? Help the children to come up with a simple plan for the family to focus on that person for the week. Have the older ones write down a few family and individual ideas.

Prayer

Today, let us pray for all who have lost their faith.

Parent: Dear Lord, Jesus, help us to be a light to others, especially those who have lost their way.

All pray: Our Father, Hail Mary, Glory Be

All Through the Day

Jesus is the light of the world!

"Remember that the Passion of Christ ends always in the joy of the Resurrection of Christ, so when you feel in your own heart the suffering of Christ, remember the Resurrection has to come—the joy of Easter has to dawn. Never let anything so fill you with sorrow as to make you forget the joy of Christ Risen."

—Mother Teresa of Calcutta

Reflection for Parents

Each day of our lives is filled with joys and difficulties and sometimes even sorrows. During the season of Lent, we zoom in on sufferings and sacrifices specifically because Our Lord has suffered so much for us. Mother Teresa reminds us that while this is true, we should never forget the joy of the resurrection too.

Family Prayer

All make the sign of the cross.

> *Parent:* Dear Lord, thank you for all you have done to enable us to strive for Heaven and its rewards. Now let us listen to these words of Blessed Mother Teresa.

A parent or child now reads the opening quotation aloud.

> *All:* Blessed Mother Mary, bring us closer to your Son, Jesus. Blessed Mother Teresa, pray for us. Amen.

A Story from Mother Teresa's Life

Because Mother Teresa worked so much with the sick and dying, permission was given to her to store lifesaving medicines at her home in Calcutta. Mother Teresa told the story about a father running into the house one day, frantically announcing that his son was dying and needed a medicine that can only be gotten in England to be able to save his life. The man was hoping that Mother Teresa would know what to do.

All kinds of medicines were delivered regularly to the house after being collected by coworkers who went house to house and gathered leftover medicines. Miraculously, as Mother Teresa was talking with the father, another man came in at that moment with a basket of medicines. Right on the top of the pile of medicines was the exact one the father needed to save his son's life.

Mother Teresa thanked God that in his providence he sent that particular medicine delivery at the precise time there was a need for it. She said that had it been underneath the pile, she may not have noticed it at that moment. Mother Teresa was convinced that God was showing everyone that he was not only taking care of that boy, but that he loves each of us with a beautiful tender concern.

Fasting

Encourage the children to fast from a treat today.

Almsgiving

Ask the children if they can draw a picture (the younger ones) or write a short uplifting poem (the older ones) that they will gift to someone this week.

Prayer

Parent: Dear Lord, Jesus, thank you for the joy of your resurrection.

All pray: Our Father, Hail Mary, Glory Be

All Through the Day

I will focus on the joy of the risen Christ even when things are tough.

"Lord, help us to see in your Crucifixion and Resurrection an example of how to endure and seemingly die in the agony and conflict of daily life, so that we may live more fully and creatively."

—Mother Teresa of Calcutta

Reflection for Parents

M other Teresa suggests we look to Jesus' crucifixion and resurrection to help us in our daily conflicts and problems. Our challenges will never come close to our Lord's pain and suffering, but we can learn from Jesus how we are to endure hardship and challenges. Mother Teresa reminds us that in gaining strength through prayer and imitation of our Savior, we will be much more fulfilled. St. Paul reminds us, "If we have grown into union with him through a death like his, we shall also be united with him in the resurrection" (Rom 6:5).

Family Prayer

All make the sign of the cross.

> *Parent*: Dear Jesus, we want to look to you for guidance and strength in all that we do. Now let us listen to these words of Blessed Mother Teresa.

A parent or child now reads the opening quotation aloud.

> *All*: Blessed Mother Mary, bring us closer to your Son, Jesus. Blessed Mother Teresa, pray for us. Amen.

A Story from Mother Teresa's Life

Mother Teresa was keenly aware of human suffering. She cautioned people when she preached that money is not enough to alleviate many kinds of pain and trouble. Money can't buy love. People need care and love, she would say. One time a man who was half-blind came to Mother Teresa and begged her to send some sisters to visit him and his wife because their children were overseas and they were very lonely. They hadn't heard the sound of another human voice in some time. They yearned for some tenderness.

Mother Teresa encouraged others to search out the poor and lonely. They may be living next door to us. She said the poor can appear very rich with material things but are hurting inside due to lack of love. She beckons us to be an instrument of Jesus' love for them.

Fasting

Encourage the children to fast from a favorite television show today or a favorite video game.

Almsgiving

Ask the children to think of a person who may be yearning for love. What can they do to be Christ-like for them? What would Mother Teresa do?

Prayer

Today, let's pray for all of the lonely people all around the world.

Parent: Dear Lord, Jesus, thank you for your tender love for our family. Help us to be an instrument of your love to others.

All pray: Our Father, Hail Mary, Glory Be

All Through the Day

I will look to Jesus for everything.

"Joy is love, the normal result of a heart burning with love. Our lamp will be burning with sacrifices made out of love if we have joy."

—Mother Teresa of Calcutta

Reflection for Parents

Mother Teresa tells us that when our lamp burns with love it will be filled with joy. Being a parent means that we will endure many sacrifices to raise our children properly. Even so, our lives will be filled with immense joy through it all knowing that we are answering our divine calling by raising little saints to heaven! How is your lamp burning? Does it need more oil? You can refuel it with extra love and prayer.

Family Prayer

All make the sign of the cross.

>*Parent*: Dear Lord, Jesus, thank you for lighting our lamps with the fire of your love. Help us radiate it out to others. Now let us listen to these words of Blessed Mother Teresa.

A parent or child now reads the opening quotation aloud.

>*All*: Blessed Mother Mary, bring us closer to your Son, Jesus. Blessed Mother Teresa, pray for us. Amen.

A Story from Mother Teresa's Life

When visiting the poor in Australia, Mother Teresa came upon an elderly man who was living by himself in a cluttered and dirty house. Mother Teresa asked if the sisters and she could visit him and clean his house and do his laundry. The man eventually accepted her kind offer.

Mother Teresa found an old oil lamp in his home that was covered with layers of dirt and cobwebs. She cleaned it off and asked the man why he didn't light the lamp. He told her that there was no reason to because no one had ever come to visit him. Mother Teresa asked him if he'd light it if the sisters came each day, and he said he absolutely would.

So, the sisters visited each day and went about their work in the man's house in a joyful way, smiling and humming. The sisters' loving hearts truly rekindled a lamp of love and joy in that man's life, which he responded to in a very happy and grateful way.

Fasting

Talk to the children about fasting from saying any unkind words.

Almsgiving

Encourage the children to do something special for a classmate, teacher, neighbor, or friend. A simple kind word or compliment can make a difference in someone's life.

Prayer

Today, let's pray for those who have lost hope or are suffering from a broken heart.

> *Parent*: Dear Lord, Jesus, we love you! Thank you for loving us and help us to bring your love to others.

> *All pray*: Our Father, Hail Mary, Glory Be

All Through the Day

I should refuel my "lamp" with love and prayer.

THURSDAY, FOURTH WEEK OF LENT

"... that we may become instruments of peace, of love, of compassion."

—Mother Teresa of Calcutta

Reflection for Parents

Mother Teresa's aspiration speaks to all parents. In raising your children, you should aspire to be instruments of peace, love, and compassion. You must always parent with love, even at the times when you feel you are going to explode! Sometimes your parental love may seem more than a bit radical to non-Christians who don't share your views in the way you care about your children's eternal salvation. And sometimes your love may seem intense to your children simply because you care so much about their salvation. Nevertheless, all is done with peace, love, and compassion—just like our Lord.

Family Prayer

All make the sign of the cross.

> *Parent*: Dear Lord, teach us to be compassionate and loving people. Now let us listen to these words of Blessed Mother Teresa.

A parent or child now reads the opening quotation aloud.

> *All*: Blessed Mother Mary, bring us closer to your Son, Jesus. Blessed Mother Teresa, pray for us. Amen.

A Story from Mother Teresa's Life

Mother Teresa many times kept company with people from numerous faiths. She took part, along with her sisters, in a variety of prayer services with Jews, Jains, Hindus, Sikhs, Anglicans,

Armenians, Baptists, Buddhists, and others, which were held in synagogues, churches, and temples.

Mother Teresa would say, "Let us pray to our common Father" and all felt included and also united in prayer. Mother Teresa often recommended that when people gathered to pray together before working with the poor that they be encouraged to pray in their particular religion. She felt that the bond of divine love would unite all who were gathered for the same reasons.

Fasting

Talk to the children about judging others and what it means. Encourage them to take a few minutes to think about whether they may be judging others in some way: by their clothes, their skin color, their attitude, and so on. Ask them to choose to fast from judging others.

Almsgiving

Encourage the children to think of someone they can be extra nice to.

Prayer

Today, let us pray for unity among peoples.

Parent: Dear Lord, Jesus, please grant us all the graces to act with love and compassion in all circumstances.

All pray: Our Father, Hail Mary, Glory Be

All Through the Day

With God's help, I will be an instrument of love, peace, and compassion.

"You accepted patiently and humbly the rebuffs of human life, as well as the tortures of your Crucifixion and Passion. Help us to accept the pains and conflicts that come to us each day as opportunities to grow as people and become more like you."

—Mother Teresa of Calcutta

Reflection for Parents

How many times in the course of just one day do we complain about little mishaps, annoyances, and sufferings? When we begin to ponder the immense tortures our Lord endured during his passion and crucifixion for all of us, we may shrink down in embarrassment. Mother Teresa's words call us to a deeper level of living and loving. She asks our Lord to help us all accept the pains and conflicts that come to us as actual blessed opportunities for grace and growth.

Family Prayer

All make the sign of the cross.

> *Parent:* Thank you, Lord Jesus for your love for us. Help us to open to your graces and love. Now let us listen to these words of Blessed Mother Teresa.

A parent or child now reads the opening quotation aloud.

> *All:* Blessed Mother Mary, bring us closer to your Son, Jesus. Blessed Mother Teresa, pray for us. Amen.

A Story from Mother Teresa's Life

Mother Teresa often preached that our Lord calls us all to be holy—not just a few select ones—but everyone. She has said that holiness lies mysteriously in all of the little details of life. We don't have to make our lives complicated or plan to do extraordinary things. We must simply live our lives the way Our Lord has intended. We must give our hearts to God and ask him to work out all of the details. We must accept all that comes to us and ask God for the grace to become holy—right in all of the little details of life.

Fasting

Encourage the children to fast from complaining today.

Almsgiving

Tell the children that for each time they complain about something today or feel as if they want to complain, they should think about a blessing they have in their life. Further, for the older children, ask them what they might do for someone who suffers in some way.

Prayer

Today, let us pray for the persecuted and tortured people all around the world.

Parent: Dear Lord, Jesus, please ease the suffering of all who are persecuted for their faith or for any reason.

All pray: Our Father, Hail Mary, Glory Be

All Through the Day

Lord, help me this day to accept everything as an opportunity for grace, especially the difficulties.

FIFTH SUNDAY OF LENT

"When our sisters were in Ceylon, a minister of state once told me something very surprising. He said, "You know Mother, I love Christ but I hate Christians." So I asked him how could that be because it is such a contradiction, since Christ and Christians are *one*. Then he answered me, "Because Christians do not give us Christ, they do not live their Christian lives to the full."

—Mother Teresa of Calcutta

Reflection for Parents

In the three gospels for this Fifth Sunday of Lent we hear the inspiring account of the raising of Lazarus (Jn 11:1–45), Jesus speaking of his coming death (Jn 12:20–33), and the story of the woman caught in adultery (Jn 8:1–11).

Jesus says in John 12, "Amen, amen, I say to you, unless a grain of wheat falls to the ground and dies, it remains just a grain of wheat; but if it dies, it produces fruit." The raising of Lazarus was a sign of this. He was not resurrected as Jesus was, but nonetheless, he was resuscitated. But this points to Jesus' rising, demonstrating the power of Christ to raise us from our sin and bring us to new life. The woman caught in adultery was also raised to a new life. Because of Jesus' love and great mercy, she was saved physically and, more importantly, was forgiven and received new life.

Mother Teresa's words talk about the need for us to live our faith every day, and Jesus tells us that "unless a grain of wheat falls to the ground and dies," it will not bear fruit. What are we to learn from this? We can turn our thoughts to Jesus' death on the cross. When troubles come our way, we can strive through prayer to die to our selves (our own desires for things, comfort, recognition, and more) in order for God's grace to work through us and touch others. We won't inspire others as a radiant example of Christianity without living our faith at all times. In fact, we turn people away from Christianity when we live a contradictory life. A deep prayer life and frequenting the sacraments fuel our desire to live holy lives and to allow God to use us even when it's challenging and difficult for us. He will grant us the graces we need. We need to ask him.

Family Prayer

All make the sign of the cross.

> *Parent*: Dear Lord, Jesus, show us how to die to self so that we may live in your love and be a radiant example of faith, hope, and love to others. Now let us listen to these words of Blessed Mother Teresa.

A parent or child now reads the opening quotation aloud.

> *All*: Blessed Mother Mary, bring us closer to your Son, Jesus. Blessed Mother Teresa, pray for us. Amen.

A Story from Mother Teresa's Life

One time, when considering what she could do that would be meaningful for her sisters, Mother Teresa decided to ask each of the communities to write down something beautiful about the sisters at their convents. She requested that the sisters send the reflections to her. Mother Teresa was overjoyed to receive the letters because she was able to see what was on the sisters' minds and in their hearts. When she sent the responses back to the convents, the sisters were surprised to hear about their fellow sisters' observations. This fostered a spirit of love and sharing among them.

Mother Teresa pointed out that we should all be willing to look for the positive in others rather than dwell on the negative aspects of everything around us. This loving spirit will certainly help to foster changes in our families and neighborhoods, all by God's grace and our willingness to be a vessel of love and care.

Fasting

Talk with the children about their fasting plans for the week. Have them write ideas on notes they can put in their lunch boxes or backpacks as a reminder.

Almsgiving

Weather permitting, perhaps you can find time to plant some flower seeds with the children and talk about how the seeds must die in the dirt to be able to produce the flowers you will enjoy later on. Plant an extra flowerpot with seeds so the children can bring it to church to be placed before a statue of Mary at the May Crowning.

Prayer

Today, let's pray for peace in the world.

All pray: Our Father, Hail Mary, Glory Be

All Through the Day

Jesus grants me the grace to live my faith fully.

MONDAY, FIFTH WEEK OF LENT

"If in the work you have difficulties and you accept them with joy, with a big smile—in this like in any other thing—they will see your good works and glorify the Father."
—Mother Teresa of Calcutta

Reflection for Parents

Sometimes Mother Teresa's advice seems overly simple or impossible to follow. But because she was a woman of deep faith and possessed a strong spirit, she based all of her teachings on a solid prayer life.

You may not be able to smile when your washing machine is overflowing, your child is throwing up, and the dog is barking because the neighbor kids are ringing the doorbell—all at once. It would seem hardly a time to smile or to be joyful. Yet Mother Teresa knew from experience that it was not only doable, but that it was also extremely beneficial. Why waste tears or time grumbling? Why not instead offer the problems and challenges to God and ask for his grace to deal with them?

While it's true we may not feel that smile broadening across our faces initially when things go wrong, with time and prayer and a better idea of the bigger picture, we can understand that we are indeed a living example to our families in how we conduct ourselves within the nitty-gritty details of everyday life. And further, hidden within the joy is the secret of eternal salvation for us and our families. It starts with a smile!

Family Prayer

All make the sign of the cross.

> *Parent*: Dear Lord, help us to find joy in each day no matter what is happening. Now let us listen to these words of Blessed Mother Teresa.

A parent or child now reads the opening quotation aloud.

> *All*: Blessed Mother Mary, bring us closer to your Son, Jesus. Blessed Mother Teresa, pray for us. Amen.

A Story from Mother Teresa's Life

Mother Teresa spoke about the unhappiness she saw on the faces of affluent people she had met who had acquired many possessions yet still did not experience a deep and lasting joy. Mother Teresa noted the sharp contrast of the "rich" with her sisters, the "poor." The sisters had given up all of their worldly belongings to embrace the austere life of being a Missionary of Charity, yet they radiated a pure joy because they became one with God.

Fasting

Ask the children to stop themselves from saying negative things today, to instead pause and think of something nice to say.

Almsgiving

Encourage the children to count their blessings—to actually sit down with paper and pencil (or crayon) and jot down all of the good things in their lives.

Prayer

> *Parent*: Dear Lord, Jesus, bring us your joy.

> *All pray*: Our Father, Hail Mary, Glory Be

All Through the Day

I will be an example of joy.

"Peace begins with a smile—smile five times a day at someone you don't really want to smile at all—do it for peace."

—Mother Teresa of Calcutta

Reflection for Parents

Even though we don't always feel like smiling, Mother Teresa suggests we smile at someone whom we don't really want to smile at—five times a day no less! Parents have their days of not feeling very smiley. I'm sure you will agree. Today, be smiley, be loving, and be joyful—especially toward someone whom you'd rather not smile at.

Family Prayer

All make the sign of the cross.

> *Parent*: Dear Lord, You give us so many reasons to smile, yet we complain and grumble so much. We're sorry for our not-so-happy attitudes sometimes. Help us to spread your love and joy and be instruments of your peace. Now let us listen to these words of Blessed Mother Teresa.

A parent or child now reads the opening quotation aloud.

> *All*: Blessed Mother Mary, bring us closer to your Son, Jesus. Blessed Mother Teresa, pray for us. Amen.

A Story from Mother Teresa's Life

One time a Hindu mother came to Mother Teresa asking for prayers and blessings for her three-year-old son who was unable to speak. Believing very much in the redemptive power in sacrifice, Mother Teresa suggested the woman give up something she really loved. The mother said she would give up chewing betel nuts, which had become almost an addiction with her. After three months, the woman returned to Mother Teresa to report that her son was speaking and that she was thankful and delighted. Her son continued to progress, and the mother took lessons to become a Catholic. Later on the father wanted to become a Catholic too.

Fasting

Encourage the children to fast from something they really enjoy today and offer a prayer to God.

Almsgiving

It's another day to give away smiles. Talk to the children about smiling at others today and about meaning it. Let them choose a combination of easy smiles and hard smiles, the hard being to smile at those who aren't necessarily smileworthy.

Prayer

Today, let us pray for all peoples that they turn away from sin and turn to God.

Parent: Dear Lord, Jesus, thank you for your love and blessings. Please grant us your grace to make a huge difference in the lives of all we meet.

All pray: Our Father, Hail Mary, Glory Be

All Through the Day

I will do my best to bring peace to others today.

"Because we cannot see Christ we cannot express our love to Him, but our neighbors we can always see, and we can do to them what, if we saw him, we would like to do to Christ."

—Mother Teresa of Calcutta

Reflection for Parents

Your children, your spouse, your relatives, and your friends are all people you can see and touch and communicate with. Do you treat them as you would treat Jesus, whom you can't see?

Jesus asks us to do just that in the Gospel of Matthew (25:31–46). He tells us that when he comes "in his glory" we will be judged by how we have loved, how we have served Jesus in one another. Mother Teresa lived her life to care for Jesus in everyone she met. Read Matthew 25:31–46 and explain it to the children.

Family Prayer

All make the sign of the cross.

>*Parent*: Dear Jesus, help us to love you in others. Now let us listen to these words of Blessed Mother Teresa.

A parent or child now reads the opening quotation aloud.

>*All*: Blessed Mother Mary, bring us closer to your Son, Jesus. Blessed Mother Teresa, pray for us. Amen.

A Story from Mother Teresa's Life

Mother Teresa and her sisters were in constant company with the poor, sick, dying, and troubled. Each day they worshipped Jesus at Mass and then went out into the streets in search for him within each human being, especially in the suffering.

As they cared for the sick and dying, they prayed for them. Mother Teresa said that visitors seemed to feel God's presence in the house and went around reverently and quietly, speaking in hushed voices. Life seems to hang by a thin thread in the home for the dying. The sisters pour their love over discarded babies and people found in the streets. They give them the chance to live, or at least to be shown love and compassion before they die. Each person is treated as a precious and unrepeatable life.

Mother Teresa and the sisters cared for each person as if he or she were Jesus Christ. We can do the same to all those who are in our lives. They may not be sick or dying, but everyone is in need of love and tenderness. God expects us to act lovingly to all.

Fasting

Ask the children to fast from bickering.

Almsgiving

Encourage the children to give some time today to brighten someone's day.

Prayer

Let us pray for the sick and dying.

> *Parent:* Dear Lord, Jesus, grant us your graces to love more sincerely.

> *All pray:* Our Father, Hail Mary, Glory Be

All Through the Day

I will treat others like Jesus.

THURSDAY, FIFTH WEEK OF LENT

"Let us radiate the peace of God and so light His light and extinguish in the world and in the hearts of all men all hatred and love for power."
—Mother Teresa of Calcutta

Reflection for Parents

Do you radiate the peace of God to your family and community? Mother Teresa suggests we all do just that, and by doing so we can help extinguish hatred and the love for power in the world. You may feel that your *little* part in radiating peace can't make much of a difference in the world. But consider this one small, seemingly frail woman, Mother Teresa, and what her one yes to God has done to change the world by opening our eyes to the poor and those in need and impressing upon us our responsibility to love with Jesus' love. Now imagine if we all did our part. No act of love or peace is ever *little*.

Family Prayer

All make the sign of the cross.

> *Parent:* Dear Lord, please open our eyes and hearts to your boundless love for us all. Now let us listen to these words of Blessed Mother Teresa.

A parent or child now reads the opening quotation aloud.

> *All:* Blessed Mother Mary, bring us closer to your Son, Jesus. Blessed Mother Teresa, pray for us. Amen.

A Story from Mother Teresa's Life

Pope John Paul II, who loved and respected Mother Teresa, invited her to be a sort of ambassador-at-large for the gospel—defending the right to life for everyone, the union of all Christians, the family as the vital unit of society, and promoting peace in the world.

Mother Teresa was known to be very blunt at times when speaking to crowds of people when she wanted to drive home an urgent need. One time in particular, she gave an address to the United Nations and wasn't worried that she was standing before world leaders. She told them that when an unborn child is killed by abortion, we are killing God. Mother Teresa told them that abortion needs to be stopped and that it is destroying peace.

Fasting

Encourage the children to think of something they can fast from today. Tell them that it would be nice if they can decide what it should be on their own.

Almsgiving

Ask the children to consider how they can be an instrument of God's peace today.

Prayer

Let us pray for all those who don't feel peace in their hearts and who don't experience it in their lives because they live in war-torn areas.

> *Parent*: Dear Lord, Jesus, thank you for your great love for our family. Help us to spread your love and peace to others.

> *All pray*: Our Father, Hail Mary, Glory Be

All Through the Day

I will pray to radiate peace.

"When we look at the Cross we know how much He loved us then—past tense; when we look at the tabernacle, we realize how much He loves us now—now."

—Mother Teresa of Calcutta

Reflection for Parents

We are getting closer to the culmination of our Lenten journey. In the days ahead during Holy Week, we will focus upon the passion and death of Jesus Christ. Our Lord's crucifixion is enfolded with such holy meaning and vast mystery. We will never fully comprehend it this side of heaven. However, through prayer and meditation, our Lord will draw us closer to the holiness of the cross.

Mother Teresa tells us that when we gaze upon the crucifix and consider the torturous pains our Lord endured for us we understand his love. We should likewise look upon the sacred host and recognize his great love for us. He has made himself really present in the Eucharist so that we can truly be united with him when we receive him in Holy Communion and when we worship him in the Blessed Sacrament in the tabernacle.

Family Prayer

All make the sign of the cross.

> *Parent:* Dear Lord, Jesus, your love for us is such an amazing gift! Thank you! Now let us listen to these words of Blessed Mother Teresa.

A parent or child now reads the opening quotation aloud.

> *All:* Blessed Mother Mary, bring us closer to your Son, Jesus. Blessed Mother Teresa, pray for us. Amen.

A Story from Mother Teresa's Life

Mother Teresa's burning desire to bring Christ's love to the whole world has resulted in many houses being established in numerous countries. In the motherhouse in Calcutta, a world map hangs on the wall encircled with a large rosary. It has this inscription: "Go and teach all nations."

Mother Teresa's love for the poor knew no limits. She even said that if there were poor on the moon, then they would go to the moon too! Because her work did not only remain in Calcutta, the world is aware of Mother Teresa's work for the poorest of the poor and instantly recognizes the sisters in their clearly identifiable white cotton sari habit (trimmed) in blue to recall the Blessed Mother). The sisters are an unmistakable sign to the world of God's love.

Fasting

Encourage the children to fast from idle chatter today. Ask them to remember God's great love for us.

Almsgiving

Recommend that the children think about how they can tangibly show God's love to someone today who may not expect it. Spend a few minutes with them helping them with ideas.

Prayer

Today let us pray for all of the unbelievers in the world.

Parent: Dear Lord, Jesus, please help us to be an example of your love to all we meet.

All pray: Our Father, Hail Mary, Glory Be

All Through the Day

Thank you, dear Lord, for your love!

PASSION (PALM) SUNDAY

"How did Jesus love us? He died on the Cross; He made himself the Bread of Life to satisfy our hunger for His love and then He made himself the hungry one so that we, you and I, can satisfy His hunger for our love. We must thank the poor for allowing us to love Jesus in them. . . ."

—Mother Teresa of Calcutta

Reflection for Parents

Palm Sunday, or Passion Sunday, is the last Sunday in our Lenten journey. It is an extremely important day on our Church's calendar because it commemorates Jesus' triumphant entry into Jerusalem to celebrate the Passover. The people of Jerusalem recognized Jesus as their king and rushed to meet him as he rode in on a donkey, laying out palm branches before him and saying, "Hosanna to the Son of David; Blessed is he who comes in the name of the Lord! Hosanna in the highest heaven!" (Mt 21:9).

Jesus riding on a donkey fulfilled a prophecy of Zechariah: "See, your king shall come to you; a just savior is he, meek, and riding on an ass, on a colt, the foal of an ass." (Zec 9:9). The donkey was a symbol of peace; the palm branches signified that a dignitary or king was arriving in triumph. Down through the ages, palm branches have represented joy and victory. They have been used in procession on Palm Sunday and distributed among the faithful to be displayed in prominent places in their homes to be used as sacramentals. They were sometimes thrown into the fire during storms and have been placed on graves, in fields, and in barns. The ashes from the burned blessed palms are used for the following Ash Wednesday's ashes.

We begin our Holy Week today with the reading of the passion at Mass and can strive to meditate upon those events throughout the week. This is a week filled with many graces and blessings, if we open our hearts to come closer to Jesus. In Mother Teresa's words, we learn that we can receive much peace in the Bread of Life, the

Eucharist. Endeavor to receive Jesus in the Eucharist as often as you can this Holy Week.

Family Prayer

All make the sign of the cross.

> *Parent:* Dear Lord Jesus, prepare our hearts for all you wish to teach us this week. Now let us listen to these words of Blessed Mother Teresa.

A parent or child now reads the opening quotation aloud.

> *All:* Blessed Mother Mary, bring us closer to your Son, Jesus. Blessed Mother Teresa, pray for us. Amen.

A Story from Mother Teresa's Life

Mother Teresa was a woman of deep prayer and a distinct understanding of the passion of Jesus. She was intimately aware of profound suffering and shared in the cross of Christ. Mother Teresa taught her sisters the deep mysteries that lie within suffering and reminded them of St. Paul's words: "Now I rejoice in my sufferings for your sake, and in my flesh I am filling up what is lacking in the afflictions of Christ on behalf of his body, which is the church" (Col 1:24).

Mother Teresa was not one to take it easy. She rose every morning at 4:30 and went immediately to the chapel to pray. She worked throughout the day serving Jesus in her sisters and the poor, and typically didn't get to bed until midnight or later. She offered everything to Jesus. Even when she was sick or feverish, it was difficult to keep her down because she was so compelled to serve the kingdom of God.

Fasting

Talk to the children about their fasting plans for this week. Impress upon them that this is indeed a very Holy Week. Ask them to do their best to please Jesus with their offerings of love and sacrifice.

Almsgiving

Write some simple ideas down on slips of paper with the children, such as "make a card for someone who is suffering," "pray three extra Hail Marys today, and ask Mary to keep you close to her Son Jesus," "be a peacemaker today," "be a cheerful giver today," and so on. Put the ideas in a jar on the kitchen counter. They can pick one each day of Holy Week and carry it out.

Prayer

Parent: Today, as we begin Holy Week, let us pray for all who are persecuted for their faith. Dear Lord, Jesus, be with them and be with me—help me to love with your love!

All pray: Our Father, Hail Mary, Glory Be

All Through the Day

"Blessed is he who comes in the name of the Lord!"

MONDAY OF HOLY WEEK

"The world is lost for want of sweetness and kindness. People are starving for love because everybody is in such a great rush."

—Mother Teresa of Calcutta

Reflection for Parents

There's no doubt that we live in a fast-paced culture. We seem so preoccupied with looking forward to the next activity that we sometimes miss the present moment. We rush past people distracted by a myriad of things swirling around our brains.

Mother Teresa lamented that too many people in our world are starving for love. Perhaps we can stop and ponder what we can do to alleviate some of that suffering and loneliness in others. It starts in the family. Mother Teresa was famous for saying, "Love begins at home." Let's be sure to slow down our pace when possible to become more attentive to the needs around us, starting in our own families.

Family Prayer

All make the sign of the cross.

> *Parent:* Dear Lord Jesus, open our hearts to hear the cries of those who need our help. Remind us that while they may look all put together, they may still be starving for love. Now let us listen to these words of Blessed Mother Teresa.

A parent or child now reads the opening quotation aloud.

> *All:* Blessed Mother Mary, bring us closer to your Son, Jesus. Blessed Mother Teresa, pray for us. Amen.

A Story from Mother Teresa's Life

The sisters and Mother Teresa often went out in the evenings to rescue the dying off the streets. One evening, they took in four people, one in a very bad state. Mother Teresa placed the poor woman in a bed and took care of her, showering her with tenderness. A beautiful smile lit up the woman's face and she gave Mother Teresa's hand a gentle squeeze, uttering the words, *thank you* as she closed her eyes for the last time.

Each encounter with the poor and dying was a uniquely remarkable experience. Yet, this time, Mother Teresa had to stop and think what she might have done if she were that woman. She said she would have cried out for attention, letting others know that she was cold, suffering, and dying. She remarked that this woman responded to her care with such a grateful love and died with a smile on her face.

Fasting

Talk to the children about fasting from rushing around today. Have them take ten minutes to pray and think of others in need.

Almsgiving

Encourage the children to be more attentive today to the needs of others. Fasting from rushing from one thing to the next will allow for more focus on others.

Prayer

Today, let's pray for the lonely and forgotten in our world, especially in our own town.

Parent: Dear Lord, Jesus, help me to love with your love!

All pray: Our Father, Hail Mary, Glory Be

All Through the Day

I will slow down and pray to love more.

TUESDAY OF HOLY WEEK

"Let us ask our Lady to make our hearts meek and humble as her Son's was. It is so easy to be proud and harsh and selfish—so easy; but we have been created for greater things. How much we can learn from our Lady!"
—Mother Teresa of Calcutta

Reflection for Parents

Raising children is serious business! Parents not only feed and clothe their offspring but also they are hugely responsible for shaping their children's consciences while going through the daily tasks of everyday life in a family.

Mother Teresa reminds us that it is so easy for us to become cruel, harsh, and selfish. Our culture today is centered on "looking out for number one." Yet, as Christian parents, we are to teach our children God's ways, not the world's. God has created us for greater things—to love and be loved—to set an example of Christian charity. Take some time to reflect upon how you can become more charitable within your family and beyond.

Family Prayer

All make the sign of the cross.

> *Parent*: Dear Lord, Jesus, help us to be more like you— meek and humble. Help our family to be more loving. Now let us listen to these words of Blessed Mother Teresa.

A parent or child now reads the opening quotation aloud.

> *All*: Blessed Mother Mary, bring us closer to your Son, Jesus. Blessed Mother Teresa, pray for us. Amen.

A Story from Mother Teresa's Life

Mother Teresa was dearly devoted to the Blessed Virgin. She prayed the rosary daily and was in constant communication with Mary. One time Mother Teresa asked a priest in Berhampur, India—where her sisters would be opening a convent—for a large statue of Mary. He had one wrapped and delivered to the railway station. Mother Teresa boarded the train with the large box containing the statue and was asked to pay the freight for the box. Savvy Mother Teresa refused to pay, telling the man in charge that she had a traveling pass that said, "Mother Teresa and a companion." Since it was the Blessed Mother's image, she insisted that the statue was her companion. Mother Teresa got away with not paying the extra fee and her large parcel "sat" on the seat next to her for the journey!

Fasting

Ask the children to fast from being harsh and selfish today, whether in their actions or in their judgments of people.

Almsgiving

Encourage the children to give three Hail Marys to the Blessed Mother today, prayed slowly and reverently, and offered for the intention of being brought closer to her Son Jesus.

Prayer

Today, let us pray for mothers all around the world in various states and circumstances.

> *Parent*: Dear Lord, Jesus, please grant mothers all over the world the graces to look to your Mother Mary for help and grace.

> *All pray*: Our Father, Hail Mary, Glory Be

All Through the Day

Dear Mary, make me meek and humble.

WEDNESDAY OF HOLY WEEK

"Make sure that you let God's grace work in your souls by accepting whatever he gives you, and giving whatever He takes from you. True holiness consists in doing God's will with a smile."

—Mother Teresa of Calcutta

Reflection for Parents

So often, people will say they know that they could become holy *if only* . . . If only they had more money, a better job, more time to pray, less suffering, and on and on. The truth of the matter is that God, who is the Divine Physician, knows exactly what we need and when we need it. He gives us endless opportunities to become holy precisely through the thick and thin of daily life—all of it.

Mother Teresa tells us that the secret to holiness is "accepting whatever he gives you, and giving whatever he takes from you," and further, to do God's will by accepting our circumstances "with a smile." Are you smiling?

Family Prayer

All make the sign of the cross.

> *Parent*: Dear Lord Jesus, please grant us the grace to recognize you right here with us throughout our daily lives. Now let us listen to these words of Blessed Mother Teresa.

A parent or child now reads the opening quotation aloud.

> *All*: Blessed Mother Mary, bring us closer to your Son, Jesus. Blessed Mother Teresa, pray for us. Amen.

A Story from Mother Teresa's Life

There was a little orphan boy wandering around the home for the dying in Calcutta. His mother had died there and he was alone, so the sisters took the boy in. The family had once been in good standing, but due to difficult circumstances had become very poor. The boy lived in the orphanage surrounded by loving care and tenderness. The tender love made up for any material need or desire he had.

When the boy grew up, he expressed his desire to become a priest. When asked why, he explained that he wanted to help orphaned children just as Mother Teresa and her sisters had helped him. He wanted to love and serve others as he had been loved and served. This young man had grown up in austere poverty and watched his mother wither away. Once well off, later downtrodden, he accepted his life, thankful for the sisters' great love and care and a chance to survive. By God's grace, he kindled a deep inner desire to become a priest and devote his life to love all those who had nothing and no one.

Fasting

Talk to the children about acceptance. Ask them to fast from complaining and being negative today. Each time they feel like complaining, they should say this quick prayer instead: "Jesus, help me."

Almsgiving

Ask the children to help a family member in some unannounced way today.

Prayer

Parent: Dear Lord, Jesus, thank you for your endless blessings and love!

All pray: Our Father, Hail Mary, Glory Be

All Through the Day

I will try to be more accepting of my circumstances—and smile!

HOLY THURSDAY

"At the foot of the Cross she became our mother also, because Jesus said when He was dying that He gave His mother to St. John and St. John to His mother. At that moment we became her children."

—Mother Teresa of Calcutta

Reflection for Parents

On this holy day when we remember the Last Supper and the institution of the Eucharist and the priesthood, take some time to meditate on the amazing significance of Holy Thursday. Mother Teresa's words speak about the Blessed Mother being a mother to us all after Jesus gave her to St. John from the cross. Ask the Blessed Mother today to mother your family and grant you the graces to more clearly understand the beauty in this day.

Family Prayer

All make the sign of the cross.

> *Parent:* Dear Jesus, help us to be attentive to the blessings of this holy day. Now let us listen to these words of Blessed Mother Teresa.

A parent or child now reads the opening quotation aloud.

> *All:* Blessed Mother Mary, bring us closer to your Son, Jesus. Blessed Mother Teresa, pray for us. Amen.

A Story from Mother Teresa's Life

When Mother Teresa first opened the home for the dying, called *Nirmal Hriday* (the Immaculate Heart of Mary), she was met with some opposition. The home was in an empty wing of a rest home for pilgrims and was given to her to use temporarily. Even though the majority of the people recognized that she was providing an invaluable service and relieving the city of the embarrassment of people dying in the street, there were a few who grumbled.

Complaints were made that she was trying to convert people to Christianity. If Mother Teresa had an opportunity to baptize a dying person who requested the sacrament, she obliged without hesitation. But her efforts to serve the poor and dying were not primarily for conversions. A political leader made a thorough inspection of the home with the intention of closing it down. But when he saw that the sisters were feeding, medicating, and cleansing the emaciated sick and dying people he changed his mind. Reporting back to the complainers, he said he would get Mother Teresa out only if they would get their own mothers and sisters to do the work the Missionaries of Charity were doing. The opposition instantly quieted.

Fasting

Encourage the children to fast from complaining today.

Almsgiving

Ask the children to give more time to God today, to spend a bit more time conversing with him and thanking him for the holiness of this day.

Prayer

Today let us pray for religious communities, priests, and missionaries.

Parent: Dear Lord, Jesus, bless us in great abundance on this holy day so we may pass on blessings to others.

All pray: Our Father, Hail Mary, Glory Be

All Through the Day

Dear Mother Mary, inspire me to care for others.

"Suffering in itself is nothing; but suffering shared with Christ's passion is a wonderful gift. Man's most beautiful gift is that he can share in the passion of Christ. Yes, a gift and a sign of his love; because this is how his Father proved he loved the world—by giving his Son to die for us."

—Mother Teresa of Calcutta

Reflection for Parents

Here we are at one of the most momentous and significant days of the entire Church calendar. How can you structure the day to please and glorify God? What are you willing to sacrifice today, *the* day of unparalleled sacrifice? Can you unite any suffering you may be experiencing with Christ's passion as Mother Teresa suggests? Think of how you might impress upon the children that this is a very holy day in which to love and serve our Lord.

Family Prayer

All make the sign of the cross.

> *Parent*: Please, dear Lord, open our hearts fully to your immense, incredible, sacrificing love for us. Now let us listen to these words of Blessed Mother Teresa.

A parent or child now reads the opening quotation aloud.

> *All*: Blessed Mother Mary, bring us closer to your Son, Jesus. Blessed Mother Teresa, pray for us. Amen.

A Story from Mother Teresa's Life

One time Mother Teresa was explaining how we are to empty ourselves of sin, jealousy, selfishness, and pride in order to be filled with God's grace. She said that even the Blessed Mother needed to actually acknowledge that she was the handmaid of the Lord before God could fill her. Mother Teresa suggested that we take some time to ponder how unlike God we are, how unloving and unforgiving we really are, and how we don't really deserve to be close to God, yet he loves us and his heart is open to embrace us, even in our sin. Mother Teresa said that Jesus is in a sense still nailed to the cross, crowned in thorns, because of our sins.

Fasting

Help the children to choose appropriate fasting for this day. Ask them to look at a crucifix and thank Jesus for his love.

Almsgiving

Is there some act of charity or mercy that you can accomplish together as a family today? Take some time to prayerfully consider this.

Prayer

Today let us pray for all of the persecuted in the world, innocent prisoners, and the guilty ones to have a conversion of heart as did St. Dismas, the good thief who hung alongside Jesus (Lk 23:39–43).

Parent: Dear Lord, Jesus, forgive us our sins.

All pray: Our Father, Hail Mary, Glory Be

All Through the Day

Jesus suffered and died a cruel death so I may live!

HOLY SATURDAY

"Silence gives us a new outlook on everything. Listen in silence, because if your heart is full of other things you cannot hear the voice of God."

—Mother Teresa of Calcutta

Reflection for Parents

Holy Saturday is all about waiting, sorrow, prayer, and silence. Jesus was crucified on Good Friday and was sealed away in the tomb. The churches are bare after having been stripped of everything. We seem to be enveloped with a muted lonely feeling, almost like what the disciples must have felt after their beloved Messiah had been put to death. They felt alone; they missed him. They were afraid. They hid in the upper room with the Blessed Mother and prayed deeply for the Holy Spirit to strengthen them.

Silence is an essential ingredient to our prayer journeys. Mother Teresa speaks about the importance of silence and prayer. Strive to find moments of silence in which to immerse your heart into prayer today. These opportunities can be found during a quiet moment, but also in the midst of commotion when you retreat to the silence of your heart and find God there.

Family Prayer

All make the sign of the cross.

> *Parent:* Dear Jesus, we long for you to "rise from the tomb" and touch our hearts with your love and peace. Now let us listen to these words of Blessed Mother Teresa.

A parent or child now reads the opening quotation aloud.

> *All:* Blessed Mother Mary, bring us closer to your Son, Jesus. Blessed Mother Teresa, pray for us. Amen.

A Story from Mother Teresa's Life

Over the years many had wondered what would happen to the Missionaries of Charity Order once Mother Teresa passed on. How could a person so full of life and zeal and an amazing influence over the world be replaced? Mother Teresa had always said, "It's all God's work." She believed that he was in charge and she was just a stubby little pencil in his hand.

Whenever she was asked what would happen after she was gone she said, "God will find another person, more humble, more faithful, more devoted, more obedient to him, and the society will go on."

Fasting and Almsgiving

Mother Teresa often preached, "We can do no great things, only small things with great love." During our prayers, fasting, and almsgiving today, let's trust God with all our seemingly small things offered to him with great love. God will do the big work with transforming hearts and souls while we are faithful to the small things of our daily lives in the family.

Prayer

In our prayers today, let's try to be still and listen for God in the silence. He has much to tell us.

Parent: Dear Lord, Jesus, forgive us our sins. Prepare our hearts for your resurrection.

All pray: Our Father, Hail Mary, Glory Be

All Through the Day

I will wait for God in the silence.

EASTER SUNDAY

"Keep the Light of Christ always burning in your heart—
for He is the Way to walk. He is the Life to live. He is the
Love to love."

—Mother Teresa of Calcutta

Reflection for Parents

Christ the Lord is risen today, Alleluia! Happy Easter! Today is
the feast of all feasts. Because Jesus rose from the dead, we are
promised the gift of new life in this world and the next. This is truly
a day of celebration—bask in it with your family, enjoy one another's company, be blessed at Mass, and celebrate with great joy! Carry
that joy into the days ahead. Strive to be a beacon of light for others
so that they may find their way to heaven one day.

Family Prayer

All make the sign of the cross.

> *Parent*: Thank you, dear Lord, for your love and the
> blessing of our Church. Now let us listen to these
> words of Blessed Mother Teresa.

A parent or child now reads the opening quotation aloud.

> *All*: Blessed Mother Mary, bring us closer to your
> Son, Jesus. Blessed Mother Teresa, pray for us. Amen.

A Story from Mother Teresa's Life

One time when Mother Teresa and a few of her nuns were traveling, the woman driver took a few moments to tell them that she
had a great love and respect for their religious order. Mother Teresa
inquired why she felt that way. The woman proceeded to tell her that
she was always impressed by the way they greeted one another. She

said it was as if they hadn't seen one another in a long time or were meeting for the first time. The love and joy that appeared to fill their embraces and greetings were astounding to this woman. The light of Christ was clear to her. It made a difference in that woman's life.

Fasting and Almsgiving

Although today is obviously not a day of fasting and almsgiving, encourage your children to retain the spirit of prayer in their hearts that they fostered throughout their Lenten journeys. Ask them to be mindful of offering little sacrifices to God in prayer no matter what day it is and to reach out to those around them in love as Mother Teresa would have them do. Little acts of service when offered with love are huge in God's eyes.

Prayer

Today let us pray for the Church, all its members, and all the hierarchy. Let us also pray that others will be inspired to come into the Catholic Church.

> *Parent*: Dear Lord Jesus, thank you for the blessing of our family and our Church. Help us to be an inspiration to others. Please let your light burn in our hearts for others to see.

> *All pray*: Our Father, Hail Mary, Glory Be

All Through the Day

Jesus Christ is risen today!

PRAYER BEFORE A CRUCIFIX

Look down upon me, good and gentle Jesus,

while before your face I humbly kneel,

and with burning soul, pray and beseech you

to fix deep in my heart lively sentiments

of faith, hope, and charity,

true contrition for my sins,

and a firm purpose of amendment,

while I contemplate,

with great love and tender pity,

your five most precious wounds,

ponder over them within me,

and call to mind the words

that David, your prophet,

said to you, my Jesus:

"They have pierced my hands and my feet,

they have numbered all my bones" (Ps 21:17–18)

Pray these prayers for the Holy Father's intentions:

Our Father . . .

Hail Mary . . .

Glory Be . . .

SUGGESTED READING

BESTERMAN, THEODORE. *Voltaire.* New York: Harcourt, Brace & World, 1969.

BROWN, ANDREW. *Livre dangereux: Voltaire's* Dictionnaire philosophique. *A Bibliography of the Original Editions and Catalogue of an Exhibition Held In Worcester College Library To Celebrate the Tercentenary of Voltaire's Birth,* with the collaboration of J. Patrick Lee, Nicholas Cronk, and Ulla Kölving. Oxford: Voltaire Foundation, 1994.

CHARTIER, ROGER. *The Cultural Origins of the French Revolution.* Trans. Lydia G. Cochrane. Durham, NC: Duke University Press, 1991.

DARNTON, ROBERT. *The Forbidden Best-Sellers of Pre-Revolutionary France.* London: HarperCollins, 1996.

———. *The Literary Underground of the Old Regime.* Cambridge: Harvard University Press, 1982.

DAVIDSON, IAN. *Voltaire In Exile: The Last Years, 1753–78.* London: Atlantic, 2004.

JONES, COLIN. *The Great Nation: France From Louis XV to Napoleon 1715–99.* New York: Columbia University Press, 2002.

KNAPP, BETTINA L. *Voltaire revisited.* New York: Twayne, 2000.

MASON, HAYDN. *Voltaire.* New York: St. Martin's Press, 1975.

PARKER, DEREK. *Voltaire: The Universal Man.* London: Sutton, 2005.

PEARSON, ROGER. *Voltaire Almighty: A Life in Pursuit of Freedom.* New York: Bloomsbury, 2005.

TODD, CHRISTOPHER. *Voltaire, Dictionnaire philosophique.* London: Grant & Cutler, 1980.

TRAPNELL, WILLIAM. *Voltaire and His Portable Dictionary.* Frankfurt: V. Klostermann, 1972.

VOLTAIRE. *Candide, Zadig, and Other Stories.* Trans. Donald M. Frame. New York: Signet Classic, 1961.

———. *Letters Concerning the English Nation.* Ed. Nicholas Cronk. Oxford: Oxford University Press, 1994.

———. *Political Writings.* Ed. David Williams. Cambridge: Cambridge University Press, 1994.

———. *Treatise on Tolerance and Other Writings.* Trans. Simon Harvey and Brian Masters. Cambridge: Cambridge University Press, 2000.

WILLIAMS, DAVID, ED. *The Enlightenment.* Cambridge: Cambridge University Press, 1999.